Patterns of Child Care Use for Preschoolers in Los Angeles County

Laura Chyu, Anne Pebley, Sandraluz Lara-Cinisomo

Prepared for the First 5 LA

LABOR AND POPULATION

The research described in this report was conducted for First 5 LA by RAND Labor and Population, a unit of the RAND Corporation.

ISBN: 0-8330-3777-3

The RAND Corporation is a nonprofit research organization providing objective analysis and effective solutions that address the challenges facing the public and private sectors around the world. RAND's publications do not necessarily reflect the opinions of its research clients and sponsors.

RAND® is a registered trademark.

Published 2005 by the RAND Corporation
1776 Main Street, P.O. Box 2138, Santa Monica, CA 90407-2138
1200 South Hayes Street, Arlington, VA 22202-5050
201 North Craig Street, Suite 202, Pittsburgh, PA 15213-1516
RAND URL: http://www.rand.org/
To order RAND documents or to obtain additional information, contact
Distribution Services: Telephone: (310) 451-7002;
Fax: (310) 451-6915; Email: order@rand.org

Preface

This report was produced as part of the First 5 LA–RAND Research Partnership. First 5 LA is the new name for the Los Angeles County Children and Families First–Proposition 10 Commission. First 5 LA was established as a result of passage of Proposition 10 in November 1998 by the voters of California. Effective January 1, 1999, Proposition 10 added a 50-cent tax to cigarettes and other tobacco products. The revenue generated from this tax was earmarked for programs that promote early childhood development for children from birth to age 5. Twenty percent of the tax dollars were allocated to the California state Proposition 10 Commission. The remaining 80 percent is distributed to individual county Proposition 10 Commissions based on the proportion of children born in each county. The Los Angeles County Board of Supervisors established the Los Angeles County Children and Families First–Proposition 10 Commission (now known as First 5 LA) in December 1998. The Commission's goal is to use the funds generated by the implementation of Proposition 10 to invest in the health and development of young children in Los Angeles County. For more information on First 5 LA, go to www.first5.org.

The RAND Corporation is a nonprofit, independent, objective, and nonpartisan research institution, which helps to improve public policy through research and analysis. Additional information on RAND and RAND research can be found at www.rand.org. The First 5 LA–RAND Research Partnership was established

- to analyze the Los Angeles Family and Neighborhood Survey (L.A.FANS) data and disseminate research findings related to policy questions surrounding school readiness, child care choices, children's health, the contribution of neighborhood characteristics to young children's well-being, and children's health insurance coverage, access, and utilization.
- to facilitate access to L.A.FANS results and other data by developing and implementing a strategy for outreach to organizations, agencies, and community groups concerned with early childhood development in Los Angeles.
- to develop standardized measures of school readiness, child care choices, and children's health that can be used in other studies and evaluations.

Under the Research Partnership, RAND Labor and Population, a unit of the RAND Corporation, and First 5 LA research staff collaborate on identifying key policy questions on which policymakers and the public need more information. Although First 5 LA also provides funding to RAND to conduct the analyses, RAND research staff carry out the analyses and are responsible for all of the findings and conclusions. Like all RAND publications, this report has been carefully reviewed for accuracy and objectivity as part of RAND's quality assurance program.

Contents

Figures

Figure 1. Percent of Children Receiving Non-Parental Child Care in Past Four Weeks

Figure 2. Number of Child Care Arrangements

Figure 3. Type of Child Care Used, by Child's Age

Figure 4. Amount of Child Care Used

Figure 5. Monthly Cost of Child Care, by Type of Care and Hours Per Week

Figure 6. Hourly Cost of Child Care, by Type of Care

Figure 7. Average Monthly Child Care Costs, by Income Level

Figure 8. Percent Using Each Type of Child Care, by Income Quartiles

Figure 9. Ratio of Children to Adults in Primary Child Care Arrangements

Figure 10. Ratio of Children to Adults, by Child Care Type and Family Income

Figure 11. Percent of Annual Income Required to Pay Average Full-Time Child Care Costs

Figure 12. Percent of Mothers Who Are Not Employed, by Family Income Category

Figure 13. Average Hourly Cost Paid for Child Care, by Family Income

Tables

Summary

This report examines patterns of child care use in 2000–2001 for children ages 0–5 who were not yet enrolled in kindergarten or first grade. Specifically, we report on whether or not non-parental child care was used, the primary type of child care used, the amount of child care used per week, the number of arrangements, the cost of care, and child-to-adult ratios in child care settings. We investigated the relationships between these child care measures and neighborhood, family, and child characteristics in Los Angeles County. We also considered the differences in child care patterns between the poorest families and others. The goal is to provide descriptive information on basic preschool child care use patterns in Los Angeles. The report is based on the results of the 2000–2001 Los Angeles Family and Neighborhood Survey (L.A.FANS), which is a representative survey of the county of Los Angeles. Below we summarize the key findings.

Use of Non-Parental Child Care. Approximately 37 percent of children ages 0 to 5 who were not currently in school received some type of regular non-parental child care in Los Angeles County in 2000–2001. Non-parental child care was most common among older preschoolers and least common among infants. Our results show that differences in maternal education and employment were strongly associated with non-parental child care. Once these two characteristics are taken into account, Latino, low-income, and foreign-born parents were about as likely to use non-parental child care as other families. Mothers employed full-time were almost 10 times as likely to use non-parental child care as mothers who were not employed. However, the use of non-parental child care was not limited to working mothers: 17 percent of mothers who were not employed used non parental child care. Conversely, not all employed mothers used non-parental child care: approximately 30 percent of children whose mothers were employed full-time received no non-parental child care. Mothers who were not married or cohabiting and teen mothers were also significantly more likely to use non-parental child care.

Primary Type of Child Care Used. Most parents reported using only one non-parental child care arrangement for their child. Among preschoolers in L.A.FANS receiving non-parental child care, relative and center care were the most common types: 37 percent used relative care, 24 percent used non-relative care, and 39 percent use center care. The type of care used varied considerably by age of the child: Children under age 1 were most likely to be cared for by relatives, while those ages 3 to 5 were most likely to have center care. Full-time maternal employment, ethnicity, marital/cohabitation status, teen motherhood, and the child's age were significantly associated with the type of child care used. Women who worked full-time used disproportionately more relative care than center care compared with women who were not employed. African-American families appeared to be *more* likely to use center-based care than white families, when other factors were held constant. Single (non-cohabiting) mothers were more likely to use non-relative care than center care compared with married women. Teen mothers use less non-relative care and more center care. Surprisingly, family income was not related to the general type of child care chosen.

There were also regional differences by service planning area (SPA) in the types of child care used. Compared with children in SPA 6 (South), children in several other SPAs were more likely to be in center-based child care and less likely to use relative or non-relative child care. This regional pattern may have been due to the characteristics of each SPA—although our analysis controls for many key characteristics—or differences in the availability of child care. These regional differences may be a particularly important focus for initiatives to expand child care and preschools.

Amount of Child Care. For preschoolers ages 0–5 in L.A.FANS, 43 percent received part-time child care (less than 30 hours per week) and 57 percent received full-time child care (30 or more hours per week). Among children receiving non-parental care, the youngest children were most likely to receive full-time care. Seventy-seven percent of children under age 1 received full-time care compared with 50 percent of children ages 3 to 5. The results of the analysis showed that, not surprisingly, mothers who were employed full-time were more likely to use full-time care for their children. Perhaps more surprising is the result that boys were more than twice as likely as girls to receive full-time child care.

Child Care Costs and Child-Adult Ratios. Our results show that child care can be a substantial portion of families' budgets. For example, families with an annual income of $13,000 or less who used full-time non-parental child care paid an average of $155 per month in child care costs. The comparable average monthly cost was $118 for families with incomes of $13,000 to $23,999; $241 for families with incomes of $24,000 to $46,999; and $396 for families with incomes of $47,000 and higher. These average costs would have been considerably higher, except that a substantial proportion of families, particularly in the lower-income groups, received child care at no cost.

Relative care was by far the least expensive type of child care. More than half of relative-provided child care was provided at no cost, but when parents paid relatives to care for their children, they paid an average of $2.54 per hour compared with $4.10 and $4.62 per hour for non-relative and center-based care.

Our multivariate results show that families were significantly more likely to pay for child care (as opposed to receiving it at no cost) if the mother had education beyond college, was employed, and was using care providers other than relatives. Moreover, families were significantly more likely to have to pay for part-time than for full-time child care. For families who did pay for child care, the multivariate results show that those who used full-time child care paid significantly less per hour than those who used part-time care. Both the greater need to pay for part-time care and its higher hourly cost suggest that finding and paying for part-time care was more difficult for families that needed part-time care providers.

We assessed child care quality using child-to-adult caretaker ratios for child care arrangements. These ratios have considerable limitations as indicators of child care quality. However, our analysis of these ratios produced several interesting results. On average, child-adult ratios were substantially higher for center-based care than for relative care. Non-relative care ratios were also higher than those for relative arrangements, but considerably below ratios for centers. An examination of the ratios by type of care and family income (see Figure 10) illustrated the diversity in the care environments within each type of care category. For example, for non-relative care, children from the poorest families were in arrangements with an average of 5.4 children per adult caretaker, whereas children from families earning more than $47,000 per year were in arrangements with ratios of 2.1. We speculate that the difference may have been due in part to the fact that non-relative arrangements used by poor families may have been more likely to be neighbors or other adults who take care of multiple children in their home while non-relative arrangements for higher-income families may have been more likely to be nannies or baby-sitters responsible only for one or two children. On the other hand, child care centers used by the highest-income group had higher child-adult ratios than those used by the lowest-income group.

Our multivariate results show that children in poor (rather than very poor) neighborhoods, younger children, and those in higher-income families were more likely to have low child-adult ratios. Holding other factors constant, we found that child-adult ratios were highest for center care and lowest for non-relative care. The cost of child care was significantly related to child-adult ratios, but the association was not as strong or consistent as might have been expected.

Poor Families and Child Care. We also examined child care use by the poorest families in the L.A.FANS sample: those with annual incomes of less than $24,000. One important difference between lower- and higher-income families was that mothers in poor families were considerably less likely to work. While approximately three-quarters of mothers in the poorest families were not employed, the comparable percentage for families with incomes above $47,000 was 34 percent. Those who did use non-parental child care rely heavily on relatives who provided care at no or low cost. Low-income families also were more likely to have free or subsidized care for their children. However, more than half of the poorest families who used child care reported paying for care and not receiving any subsidy.

Discussion. The results in this report show that child care use patterns in 2000–2001 varied considerably for preschoolers of different ages. Maternal education and work status played a major role in determining the type of care children received in their first five years of life. There were substantial variations across regions in the proportion receiving non-parental child care. Non-parental child care costs were high relative to family income, particularly for poor families.

CHAPTER ONE
Introduction

Since the 1960s, women's participation in the labor force has increased markedly. As a result, the number of young children whose mothers are employed has also increased (Hofferth, 1996). Women's employment, combined with changing family structure and parents' wishes to give their young children educational experience and socialization in a structured setting, has led to a dramatic increase in the demand for and use of non-parental child care. National data from 2001 show that 61 percent of children age 6 and younger who are not yet in kindergarten participated in some type of non-parental child care or early childhood education program (Federal Interagency Forum on Child and Family Statistics, 2004). Since the late 1990s, the demand for child care among poor families has also increased as welfare reform has encouraged mothers of young children to move into the labor force (Loeb et al., 2004).

Strictly speaking, child care and early childhood education are distinct concepts. "Child care" refers to arrangements for individuals, generally adults, to look after children and respond to their needs, regardless of whether the care includes any explicit educational content. For example, a woman may provide child care for her neighbor's child simply by having the child in her home and attending to the child's basic needs. By contrast, early childhood education programs, of which preschools and prekindergartens are a part, provide care for children but also include significant and explicit educational or learning content as part of their regular activities. For example, activities may include drawing, reading stories, learning letters and numbers, etc. In practice, it is often difficult to distinguish between early childhood programs and other types of child care. Early child care education programs are often located in child care centers and, to a lesser extent, in family child care homes (Malaske-Samu and Muranaka, 2000; Jacobson et al., 2001; Loeb et al., 2004) rather than being identified separately as early childhood education facilities or preschools. Moreover, the educational content and quality of preschools and other explicitly education-oriented child care can vary considerably (Loeb et al., 2004). For this reason, in this report we do not attempt to distinguish between early childhood education programs and other types of child care. We use the term "child care" to refer to all types of child care. Because preschools and child care centers often offer similar types of programs, we group them together as "center-based care."

There is ample evidence that the quality of child care for young children has an important impact on their development (Howes and Hamilton, 1993; Howes and James, 2002; Duncan et al., 2003). High-quality child care increases children's language development, self-confidence and emotional security, and ability to regulate their own behavior (Howes and Hamilton, 1993), all of which are essential for school readiness (National Research Council, 2001) and other aspects of children's lives. Moreover, recent research in neurobiological and behavioral sciences has demonstrated that children's brain development is dependent not only on genetic inheritance but also on interaction with the social, cognitive, and physical environment in which children live—particularly during gestation and early childhood (Shonkoff and Phillips, 2000). A recent report from the National Academy of Sciences on this new brain development research concludes that recent scientific advances have

...generated a much deeper appreciation of: (1) the importance of early life experiences, as well as the inseparable and highly interactive influences of genetics and environment, on the development of the brain and the unfolding of human behavior; (2) the central role of early relationships as a source of either support and adaptation or risk and dysfunction; (3) the powerful capabilities, complex emotions, and essential social skills that develop during the earliest years of life; and (4) the capacity to increase the odds of favorable developmental outcomes through planned interventions (Shonkoff and Phillips, 2000; pp. 1–2).

High-quality child care appears to be especially important for children from disadvantaged backgrounds, because these programs can supplement poor home environments through greater exposure to reading, books, and problem solving and by helping children learn to regulate their own behavior (Phillips et al., 1994; Howes and James, 2002; Currie, 2000). Children who live in poverty and whose parents are poorly educated are particularly vulnerable to behavior problems and delayed development of basic skills (Brooks-Gunn and Duncan, 1997; Bradley and Corwyn, 2002). Part of the reason may be the quality of the home environment: In an earlier report on Los Angeles County, we showed that poor maternal education and living in poor neighborhoods made it less likely that children were read to or visited the library regularly (Lara-Cinisomo and Pebley, 2003).

Public Policy

The increasing demand for child care coupled with new research on the importance of early childhood environments for learning and brain development have made child care and early childhood education major public policy issues at all levels of government. In April 1997, the Clinton administration held a high-profile national conference known as *The White House Conference on Early Childhood Development and Learning: What New Research on the Brain Tells Us About Our Youngest Children.* They also launched several early childhood education initiatives. The Bush administration has followed up with its own national conference and the Early Childhood Education Initiative headed by First Lady Laura Bush. At the local level, many states provide child care subsidies both with federal funds and their own funds (Loeb et al., 2004; Blau, 2001) and are working to increase child care quality through licensing and provider education programs. For example, the California Department of Education (CDE) provides funding for child care for children whose parents are poor, migrant farm workers, students, Native Americans, and CalWORKS recipients.

Until the recent downturn in the economy, the state of California invested heavily in child care programs. For example, state funding for child care increased by $800 million in 1996 to $3.1 billion in the 2002–2003 fiscal year (Fuller and Huang, 2003).[1] However, research by Fuller and colleagues (Fuller and Huang, 2003; Fuller et al., 2002) shows that this increase in funding had only a small effect on the number of center-based child care and preschool slots available in California. The investment in center and preschool slots is particularly important because preschools and centers are more likely to include education-related activities than other types of child care (Loeb et al., 2004). Instead of increasing the availability of center-based care, most of the funding went to non–center-based child care, such as licensed family child care homes (FCCHs), in the form of child care subsidies to providers. In fact, in Los Angeles County, the growth in center-based slots per 100 children ages 0 to 5 between 1996 and 2000 was essentially zero (Fuller et al., 2002).

---

[1] Funding for child care decreased in the 2003–2004 fiscal year to $2.2 billion (California Department of Education, 2004) because of the state's budget crisis.

The increased emphasis on the importance of early childhood education in the past decade has led several states, counties, and cities to expand or propose expansion of publicly funded early childhood education programs (Fuller and Huang, 2003; Herszenhorn, 2004; McCrary and Condrey, 2003; Andrade, 2002). These early childhood programs are usually directed to 3- and 4-year-olds and take the form of preschools or prekindergartens, often tied to or run by the local school system. For example, Georgia uses money from the state lottery to finance universal preschool open to all 4-year-olds. By 2002, virtually all of Georgia's school districts were participating in the plan and more than 50 percent of eligible children were enrolled (Andrade, 2002).

Following in the footsteps of programs outside of California, the Los Angeles County First 5 Commission (known as First 5 LA) launched a major effort in 2002 to design and fund a high-quality, voluntary preschool program for all 4-year-olds in the county. First 5 LA has provided an initial allocation of $600 million to begin implementation of the universal preschool (UPS) plan. The plan is designed to build on current infrastructure, including child care centers, existing preschools, and other early childhood educational resources. More information on the UPS plan is available at http://www.first5.org/ourprojects/universalaccess.php4.

Objective and Organization of This Report

As background to the launch of the UPS plan by First 5 LA and other policy initiatives related to expanding child care options and early childhood education, First 5 LA asked the RAND Corporation to investigate basic patterns of child care use for children age 5 and younger in Los Angeles County as part of the First 5 LA–RAND Research Partnership. Specifically, First 5 LA is interested in the patterns of child care use among major social groups in Los Angeles, including socioeconomic groups, ethnic communities, and foreign and native-born parents. This report is intended to provide a broad overview of patterns of child care use on which new initiatives to expand child care and preschool can build.

In this report, we use data from the Los Angeles Family and Neighborhood Survey (L.A.FANS) to examine patterns of child care use in Los Angeles County. We present results on several aspects of child care patterns. Specifically, we examine whether or not each child receives any type of non-parental child care on a regular basis, the primary type of care used, the number of hours the child spends in non-parental care, the number of child care arrangements a child has, the costs of child care, and child-adult ratios in child care settings. We examine the relationship between each of these aspects of child care and maternal and child characteristics for children age 5 and younger who are not yet enrolled in kindergarten or elementary school.

Our report is organized as follows: Chapter Two provides a brief overview of the L.A.FANS study and outlines the child care measures collected by L.A.FANS. The results of our analysis are presented in Chapter Three. In the analysis, we examine the association between child care patterns and key geographic, socioeconomic, and demographic characteristics. The specific variables included in the analysis were chosen primarily because they represent major socioeconomic and demographic groups of interest to policymakers in Los Angeles County. Most of these characteristics have also been shown in previous research to be associated with the use of non-parental child care (Hofferth and Wissoker, 1992; Hofferth, 1996). At the neighborhood level, we look at differences by service planning areas (SPAs)— which represent geographic regions of Los Angeles County—and neighborhood poverty levels. At the family level, we examine the relationship of child care with maternal education, work status, income, race/ethnicity, maternal nativity status, marital status, and whether the mother was a teenager when she had the child. We also look at differences in child care by children's age and sex.

We conducted two types of analysis. First, we use bivariate tabulations to examine child care characteristics by each geographic, socioeconomic, and demographic variable. This analysis will be useful to organizations, groups, and individuals who are seeking information about child care use patterns among social groups in which they have a particular interest. For example, organizations working with foreign-born parents may be especially interested in knowing what types of child care these parents use.

Second, we examined the relationship between child care and all the geographic, socioeconomic, and demographic variables combined using multivariate statistical methods. These statistical techniques allow us to look at the effect of each variable on child care while holding constant the effects of all other geographic, socioeconomic, and demographic variables. In other words, these results show the association between child care and each variable *net* of the effects of other variables. This analysis is important for understanding which of the independent variables we include are the most important predictors of child care variables.

Chapter Four focuses on child care use by poorer families in the sample and investigates how they pay for child care. Low-income families are of particular interest to policymakers because they are least able to afford high-quality child care. Finally, Chapter Five summarizes the main conclusions of the report.

CHAPTER TWO

Los Angeles Family and Neighborhood Survey (L.A.FANS)

Survey Design

L.A.FANS is a study of the effects of neighborhood social conditions and family life on the growth and development of children. The L.A.FANS data is designed for multilevel analyses including neighborhood level and family level analyses. The project is a collaboration of a multidisciplinary team of researchers at the RAND Corporation, UCLA, and several other universities nationwide. Funding was provided primarily by the National Institutes of Health.

L.A.FANS is based on a sample of 65 neighborhoods (defined in L.A.FANS as census tracts) selected from the 1,652 census tracts in Los Angeles County. The sample was based on a stratified sampling design in which poor neighborhoods and households with children were oversampled relative to their proportion in the population. Interviews were conducted in 2000–2001. When the results are adjusted for the oversampling, the L.A.FANS sample is representative of the population of Los Angeles County. The response rates for the survey were 89 percent for mothers and 87 percent for children. These response rates are equal to or better than response rates in high-quality national sample surveys (Sastry et al., 2003).

Within each of the 65 neighborhoods, households were sampled randomly (with the oversamples noted above). For each household, one adult was chosen at random by computer to provide basic social and demographic information on household members. One resident child (age 0 to 17) was selected at random by computer to participate in the study. If the sampled child had siblings under age 18 living in the household, one of them was also randomly sampled.[2] Each child's primary caregiver (generally his/her mother) was also interviewed. Since primary caregivers were almost always mothers, we refer to them as mothers throughout this report. The sample for this report consists of 887 children ages 0 to 5 who are not yet enrolled in school (including kindergarten) and for whom complete data are available.

Table 1 provides basic characteristics of L.A.FANS neighborhoods from the 2000 census data for very poor, poor, and nonpoor neighborhoods,[3] included in the L.A.FANS sample. The fourth column of the table provides results for all L.A.FANS tracts combined and the final column shows results for all Los Angeles County census tracts combined. When compared with the numbers in the second-to-last column, the numbers in the last column show that the L.A. FANS data, when adjusted for oversampling, closely match the figures for Los Angeles County as a whole.

---

[2] In this report, we include both the sampled child (RSC) and his/her randomly sampled sibling (SIB) if two children were chosen as respondents within the household. Only 10 percent of the RSCs in the sample also had a SIB in the sample for this analysis. The L.A.FANS sampling weights used in this analysis account for the sampling design, non-response, and multiple children per household. We also use statistical procedures in multivariate models which correct for clustering within neighborhoods. We experimented with standard error corrections for multiple children per household, but found that they did not change the results presented here.

[3] Census tracts in Los Angeles County were divided into these three groups based on the percent of the population in poverty in 1997. The percent in poverty was an estimate made by the L.A. County Urban Research Division. Very poor tracts are those in the highest 10 percent of the distribution. Poor tracts are those in the next highest 30 percent, and nonpoor tracts are those in the lowest 60 percent of the poverty distribution. For more details, see Sastry et al. (2003).

However, the percent white and the median household income in the L.A.FANS sample are slightly higher than the comparable figures for Los Angeles County.

Table 1. Characteristics of Neighborhoods Included in L.A.FANS

	Very Poor Neighbor-hoods	Poor Neighbor-hoods	Nonpoor Neighbor-hoods	Total for All L.A.FANS Tracts[4]	Total for All L.A. County Tracts
Characteristic					
Number of census tracts	20	20	25	65	1,652
% Population foreign born	49	49	26	34	35
% Population who are recent immigrants (since 1990)	21	18	7	11	12
Residential stability (% Population in same house five years ago)	48	49	53	52	53
% households with income <$15k	35	21	11	16	17
% households with income >=$75k	7	13	35	27	25
Median household income	$23,391	$33,854	$55,378	$46,981	$42,189
% Families who are poor (below the federal poverty line)	39	24	10	16	17
% Female-headed single-parent households	16	10	6	8	8
% White	4	14	48	36	31
% African-American	16	6	7	7	9
% Latino	69	64	24	38	45
% Asian and Pacific Islanders	4	9	16	13	12
% Other ethnic groups	6	7	5	6	3
% of L.A. County Neighborhoods in this category	9	34	56	--	--

Source: All data come from the 2000 U.S. Census.

As shown in Table 1, about half of the population of very poor and poor neighborhoods and about a third of the population of all L.A.FANS neighborhoods were born outside the United States, reflecting the demographic composition of Los Angeles County. However, the majority of foreign-born residents came to the United States before 1990. For example, in very poor neighborhoods, 49 percent of residents were foreign born, but only 21 percent came to the United States after 1990.

Table 1 also shows the residential stability, or the degree to which residents move in and out, of each neighborhood. Residential stability appears to be important for the development of stable and healthy communities for children (Sampson, Morenoff, and Gannon-Rowley, 2002). Residential stability was only slightly higher in nonpoor neighborhoods than in the poorer ones: Roughly half of residents in each group of neighborhoods lived in the same dwelling unit in 1995 that they were occupying in 2000.

Not surprisingly, the three groups of neighborhoods differed dramatically in median household income and in the proportion of households who were very poor (defined here as having incomes below $15,000 per year) or relatively well-off (defined here as having incomes of $75,000

---

[4] These averages were weighted to correct for oversampling and thus represent L.A. County as a whole.

per year or more). We also show the proportion of households in each group of neighborhoods who were below the federal poverty line. This proportion varied from 39 percent in very poor neighborhoods to 10 percent in nonpoor neighborhoods.

Female-headed single parent families are more likely to be poor and to face greater time constraints than families with two parents (McLanahan and Sandefur, 1994). Table 1 shows that female-headed single-parent families were more common in very poor than nonpoor neighborhoods in Los Angeles County.

The ethnic composition of neighborhoods varied considerably by poverty status. Very poor neighborhoods were predominantly Latino and African-American. Nonpoor neighborhoods were predominantly white, Latino, and Asian. Residents in the "other" ethnic groups include Native Americans, multiethnic individuals, and those who preferred not to report ethnicity. This sample did not have sufficient numbers of Native American or multiethnic respondents for us to analyze them separately, and thus were not included in the analysis.

In Table 2, we provide the weighted percentage distribution of cases in our sample by the neighborhood, family, and child characteristics examined in this report. The results we report are often stratified by age of the child, because children at different ages have different developmental and child care needs. For example, babies under age 1 require considerably more care and specialized tasks, such as diaper changes. Therefore, Table 2 also shows the distributions for each age group used in the report (i.e., under 1 year, 1 to 2 years, 3 to 5 years) as well as for all age groups combined. The bottom row of the table shows the unweighted number of cases for each age group. Below, we discuss only the results for the total sample for the sake of brevity.

The results in Table 2 reflect differences in the age distribution and birth rates among different groups in the Los Angeles County population. For example, only 4 percent of the total sample ages 0 to 5 was located in SPA 5 (West). By contrast, between 16 and 18 percent of the sample was in each of SPAs 2, 3, 7, and 8. The reason is that the age structure was considerably older in SPA 5 and the proportion of families with young children was considerably smaller. The majority of children under 5 lived in nonpoor neighborhoods and were Latino. Their mothers were more likely to not be employed, to be U.S. born, to be married, and not to have been teenage mothers. Relatively few of children's mothers graduated from college or attended school after college, but a majority graduated from high school and/or attended some college. As in the population as a whole, slightly more children in the weighted sample were girls.

Table 2. Sample Distribution, by Characteristics (Weighted Percentages)

	Under 1 Year	1 to 2 Years	3 to 5 Years	Total
Service Planning Area (SPA)				
Antelope Valley (SPA 1)	9	11	8	9
San Fernando (SPA 2)	10	16	20	17
San Gabriel (SPA 3)	15	21	16	18
Metro (SPA 4)	12	6	11	9
West (SPA 5)	5	5	3	4
South (SPA 6)	9	8	9	8
East (SPA 7)	18	19	17	18
South Bay (SPA 8)	22	14	17	16
Neighborhood Poverty Level				
Very poor	19	14	15	15
Poor	36	36	35	35
Nonpoor	45	50	51	50
Family Income[5]				
First (lowest) quartile	23	25	19	22
Second quartile	20	23	25	24
Third quartile	29	25	28	27
Fourth (highest) quartile	28	27	27	27
Maternal Education				
Less than high school	37	34	37	36
High school graduate	21	21	20	21
Beyond high school	21	29	25	26
College graduate	11	11	12	11
Beyond college	10	5	5	6
Employment Status[6]				
Not employed	58	62	57	59
Part-time	16	11	14	13
Full-time	26	27	29	28
Ethnicity				
White	19	23	19	21
Latino	61	55	60	58
Black	10	9	11	10
Asian/Pacific Islander	10	13	10	11
Maternal Nativity Status				
U.S. born	66	57	55	57
Foreign born	34	43	45	43
Marital Status				
Married	65	62	64	63
Single (not Married/not cohabitating)	9	22	22	20
Cohabitating (not married)	26	16	15	17
Teenage Mother[7]				
Yes	2	4	2	3
No	98	96	98	97
Child's Gender				
Male	51	45	53	49
Female	49	55	47	51
Unweighted number of cases	157	330	368	855

---

[5] This panel excludes 13 cases with missing income information.
[6] Part-time employment is defined as those working 34 hours per week or less. Full-time employment status includes those working 35 hours or more.
[7] Teenaged mothers are defined as those age 17 and younger at the time their child was born.

L.A.FANS Child Care Measures

The L.A.FANS survey collected current child care information for all sampled children who had not yet completed elementary school. In this report, we focus on children age 5 and younger who were not yet in kindergarten or first grade. Mothers were asked to report about the three most common non-parental child care arrangements that their child used in the four weeks before the survey. L.A.FANS did not ask about periods of time in which children were cared for by their own parents, although the questions did include care by other relatives (e.g., siblings, grandparents, aunts). Respondents who did not include Head Start on the initial list of child care arrangements were also asked whether or not their child had attended Head Start in the four-week reference period.

In this study, we examine several facets of child care, including

- whether or not the child was in non-parental child care during the four weeks before the interview;
- the primary type of child care used;
- the number of hours children spent in non-parental child care arrangements each week;
- the number of child care arrangements used during the four-week period;
- the costs of child care; and
- child-adult ratios in the child care setting.

These questions were asked in the child care section of the L.A.FANS Parent questionnaire. All data were reported by the child's primary caregiver, typically mothers. For a list of questions asked, see Appendix A. The questionnaire is at www.lasurvey.rand.org.

Child care variables used in this report are as follows:

Regular Use of Child Care. Regular use of non-parental child care is child care (aside from occasional baby-sitters) not provided by the child's parents which was used during the four weeks before the interview. Child care in this study is defined to include any form of regular non-parental care.

Primary Type of Child Care. Mothers were asked to identify the child care arrangement used most frequently. Non-parental child care is divided into three main categories: (1) relative care, (2) non-relative care, and (3) center-based care. These categories are based on those used in previous studies on child care (NICHD Early Child Care Research Network, 1997; Hofferth and Wissoker, 1992; Gordon and Chase-Lansdale, 2001). We combine non-relative care in the child's home with non-relative care in the provider's home, and we exclude parental care. Relative care includes any care by relatives other than the child's parents (e.g., by grandparents, siblings, aunts, and uncles). Non-relative care is care provided by a regular baby-sitter, day care provider, maid, nanny, au pair, neighbor, or friend, and could take place in the child's or the provider's home. Center-based care included day care centers, nursery schools, preschools, and Head Start programs.

Because only approximately 5 percent of the sample reported participation in Head Start programs, they were included in the general center care category.[8]

Amount of Child Care Used Per Week. The amount of child care was measured as the average number of hours that the child was in non-parental care per week (for all non-parental child care arrangements combined) during the four weeks before the interview. Amount of care is categorized as (1) 1–30 hours per week and (2) 30 or more hours per week. This categorization was drawn from the NICHD Study of Early Child Care, which found this breakdown to be associated with the frequency of behavioral problems among children 4–5 years old (Peth-Pierce, 1998).

Number of Arrangements Used. Mothers were asked about the number of non-parental child care arrangements used. A vast majority (86 percent) reported using only one primary type of care arrangement on a regular basis. Although a 1995 nationwide study showed that a large proportion of the sample used multiple child care arrangements (Smith, 2000), the difference is primarily due to the fact that this study included parental care as a separate child care arrangement while we focus exclusively on non-parental care.

Cost of Care. Mothers were asked how much each child care arrangement costs, and whether these costs were paid by themselves or by someone else. In this report, we examine the monthly and hourly costs of child care by type of care and by socioeconomic, demographic, and geographic characteristics.

Child-Adult Ratios. Measurement of the quality of child care is complex (Howes and James, 2002) and difficult to assess in a sample survey of parents. In this study, we measure one basic aspect of child care quality for each type of care: the ratio of children to adult caretakers in the child care arrangement. In general, a lower ratio of children to caretakers is an indicator of higher-quality child care. However, readers should keep in mind that these ratios do not measure other aspects of child care quality that may be more important, such as whether child care activities include stimulating environments and activities that help children develop cognitive, social, and academic skills (e.g., number and letter recognition).

---

[8] It is possible that some parents reported participation in Head Start as a center-based child care arrangement rather than specifying Head Start per se.

CHAPTER THREE
Results

In this chapter, we examine the association between geographic, socioeconomic, and demographic characteristics and child care patterns. Because children at different ages require different kinds of care and costs are typically associated with type of care, most results are presented separately for children in three age groups based on developmental stages: less than 1 year (infants), 1–2 years, and 3–5 years. These age groups are 19 percent, 38 percent, and 43 percent (unweighted percentages), respectively, of the sample of children under 5 that is included is this report.

As described previously, we conducted two types of analysis. The first is bivariate tabulations. This analysis will be useful to organizations, groups, and individuals who are seeking information about child care use among social groups in which they have a particular interest. All results were weighted using weights provided by L.A.FANS, unless otherwise specified.

Many of the independent variables in the analysis (i.e., geographic, socioeconomic, and demographic characteristics) are likely to be interrelated. For example, foreign-born parents are generally more likely to live in lower-income neighborhoods and have lower levels of educational attainment than U.S.-born parents. Therefore, we also carried out a second type of analysis using multivariate regression models. These multivariate results allow us to look at the effect of each variable on child care while controlling for or holding constant the effects of all other geographic, socioeconomic, and demographic variables. For example, we can assess whether differences by ethnicity or nativity status remain significant once we hold income constant. In other words, are the apparent effects of ethnicity or nativity status really the result of differences by ethnicity and nativity in family income? This analysis is useful in understanding which of the independent variables we include were the most important predictors of child care patterns.

Regular Use of Non-Parental Child Care

We begin by examining the proportion of children who received regular non-parental care during the four weeks preceding the survey. Figure 1 below shows the proportion of young children in three age groups who received non-parental care during this period. Thirty-seven percent of all children age 5 and younger received non-parental child care. Not surprisingly, the portion using child care varied considerably with age: Only 22 percent of infants (under 1 year) used child care compared with about 40 percent of older children.

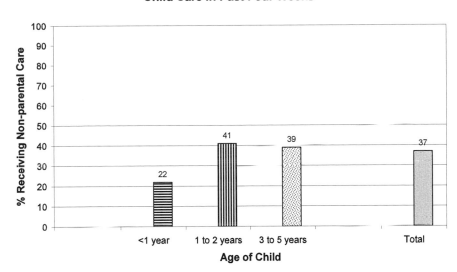

Figure 1. Percent of Children Receiving Non-parental Child Care in Past Four Weeks

As Table 3 shows, the use of child care varied among families, neighborhoods, and children with different characteristics. The number of cases for some of the age-specific samples is relatively small. In particular, there are only 166 children under age 1 included in the analysis. Therefore, the results for this particular age group should be interpreted cautiously.

For reasons of sample size, we focus our discussion primarily on the results for the total sample 0–5 shown in the last column in Table 3. We tested the statistical significance of each variable for the total sample, by using bivariate logit analysis[9] including the categories of each individual variable (i.e., only a single variable—or dummy variables representing the categories of that variable—plus an intercept, were included in the model). We used an F-test to test the statistical significance of each variable. For categorical variables, this F-test tests the *joint* significance of all categories of the variable combined. As reflected in the discussion below, we also examined t-tests for individual coefficients for categorical variables.

---

[9] We chose this approach over X^2 or multiple paired t-tests because it is more parsimonious than paired t-tests, a stronger test than a X^2, and more consistent with the multivariate approach we use later in the paper.

Table 3. Percent of Children Receiving Non-Parental Child Care, by Child's Age[10]

	Under 1 Year	1 to 2 Years	3 to 5 Years	Total
Service Planning Area (SPA)				
Antelope Valley (SPA 1)	0	26	42	28
San Fernando (SPA 2)	16	51	47	45
San Gabriel (SPA 3)	26	44	35	38
Metro (SPA 4)	9	56	45	41
West (SPA 5)	40	57	78	60
South (SPA 6)	26	35	49	40
East (SPA 7)	22	37	52	41
South Bay (SPA 8)	25	41	49	40
Neighborhood Poverty Level				
Very poor	37	33	39	37
Poor	19	40	41	37
Nonpoor	15	47	52	44
Annual Family Income				
Less than $13,000	18	28	34	29
$13,000 to $23,999	10	31	39	31
$24,000 to $46,999	29	44	38	39
$47,000 or higher	21	62	69	59
Maternal Education				
Less than high school	14	36	34	31
High school graduate	3	30	40	29
Beyond high school	45	56	59	56
College graduate	21	51	61	51
Beyond college	25	55	70	53
Employment Status[11]				
Not employed	4	21	29	22
Part-time	27	65	65	57
Full-time	56	79	72	72
Ethnicity				
White	30	46	68	52
Latino	19	34	37	33
Black	27	60	57	53
Asian/Pacific Islander	6	57	49	47
Mother's Nativity				
Foreign born	17	37	37	34
U.S. born	26	49	58	50
Marital Status				
Married	19	38	48	39
Single (not married/not cohabitating)	62	62	52	57
Cohabitating (not married)	7	34	29	26
Teenage Mother[12]				
Yes	0	75	44	40
No	21	41	46	57
Child's Gender				
Male	21	37	48	39
Female	20	49	45	42
Unweighted number of cases	157	330	368	855

---

[10] Sample for this table includes children who do and do not regularly receive some form of non-parental child care.

[11] Part-time employment is defined as those working 34 hours per week or less. Full-time employment status includes those working 35 hours or more.

[12] Teenaged mothers are defined as those 17 and younger at the time their child was born.

For the total sample of children ages 0 to 5, the statistical tests show that most of the neighborhood, family, and child characteristics were statistically significantly associated with use of non-parental child care. The associations which were not statistically significant were those between child care use and Service Planning Areas (SPAs), neighborhood poverty, whether or not the mother was a teenager (<= 17 years) when she had this child, and the child's sex.

These bivariate results show that more educated, U.S.-born, employed mothers and mothers from higher-income families were more likely to use non-parental child care for their young children. There were also some ethnic differences in child care use. In particular, Latino mothers were significantly less likely to use non-parental child care.[13] Marital and cohabitation status was also significantly related to use of child care. Mothers who were neither married nor cohabiting were significantly more likely to use non-parental care compared with other mothers.[14] Children were significantly less likely to receive non-parental care before their first birthday compared with older children.[15]

To assess the relative importance of each neighborhood, family, and child characteristic as a predictor of child care use, we estimated a multivariate statistical model that includes all the variables shown in Table 3 simultaneously. The results of this analysis provide information on the effect of each characteristic *net* of the other variables. For example, the analysis lets us examine the effects of maternal education once differences in employment status and income between poorly educated mothers and well-educated mothers are taken into account. Because the child care variable in this case is whether or not the child received any non-parental child care (i.e., it has two categories), we use a binomial logistic regression. The results of this multivariate analysis are shown in Table 4. This table presents odds-ratios, which are the odds of using child care compared with others in the sample. All characteristics in the model except family income are categorical. For these variables, the odds-ratio shows the odds of using non-parental child care compared with the reference category (also known as the omitted category) for the variable. For example, the reference category for neighborhood poverty level is "very poor." In Table 4, the odds-ratio for children in nonpoor neighborhoods shows that they were 1.24 times as likely to use non-parental child care as children in very poor neighborhoods. The odds-ratio for family income shows how much the likelihood of using non-parental child care increases for each additional dollar of income the family makes. Family income is included as a continuous variable. To make it clear that the odds-ratios are relative to the reference category, we have included a value of 1.00 in the table for the reference category. Statistically significant coefficients and odds-ratios are shown in bold.

---

[13] Both the F-test for all categories of ethnicity combined and the t-test for the individual coefficient for Latinos were statistically significantly different from zero (with whites as the reference category). No other ethnic differences were statistically significant in this bivariate analysis.

[14] Both the F-test for all categories of marital/cohabitation status and the t-test for the individual coefficient for not married/not cohabiting were statistically significant.

[15] Both the F-test for all categories of child's age and the t-test for the individual coefficient for age less than 1 year were statistically significant.

Table 4. Regular Use of Child Care: Odds-Ratios from Binomial Logistic Regression*

Variable	Odds-Ratios
Service Planning Area (SPA)	
Antelope Valley (SPA 1)	0.93
San Fernando (SPA 2)	1.24
San Gabriel (SPA 3)	0.84
Metro (SPA 4)	0.93
West (SPA 5)	1.43
South (SPA 6) *Reference category*	*1.00*
East (SPA 7)	1.14
South Bay (SPA 8)	1.02
Neighborhood Poverty Level	
Very poor *Reference Category*	*1.00*
Poor	0.90
Nonpoor	0.95
Family Income (in $10,000s)	1.01
Maternal Education	
Less than high school *Reference Category*	*1.00*
High school graduate	0.64
Beyond high school	1.41
College graduate	1.05
Beyond college	0.98
Employment Status	
Not employed *Reference category*	*1.00*
Part-time	**5.11**
Full-time	**9.67**
Ethnicity	
White *Reference category*	*1.00*
Latino	**0.57**
Black	1.20
Asian/Pacific Islander	0.74
Maternal Nativity Status	
U.S. born	0.99
Foreign born *Reference category*	*1.00*
Marital Status	
Married *Reference category*	*1.00*
Single (not married/not cohabitating)	**2.98**
Cohabitating (not married)	0.74
Teenage Mother	
Yes	**2.98**
No *Reference category*	*1.00*
Child's Age	
Under 1 year *Reference category*	*1.00*
1 to 2 years	**3.69**
3 to 5 years	**4.27**
Child's Gender	
Male	1.21
Female *Reference category*	*1.00*
Unweighted number of cases	855

* Statistically significant results (at p<.05) in bold. Reference categories in italics. Standard errors are adjusted for cluster by neighborhood.

The results show that there were no statistically significant differences in the odds of using non-parental child care by SPA, neighborhood poverty level, family income, maternal education, ethnicity, maternal nativity, or the child's gender. This means that, when other variables in the model were held constant, children whose parents were foreign born and natives, children in each ethnic group, and children in poor and well-off families were about equally likely to use non-parental child care.

On the other hand, mothers who worked, who had their child when they were teenagers, who were single (neither married nor cohabiting), and whose children were over age 1 were significantly more likely to use non-parental care. Not surprisingly, these results suggest that parents used child care more often when they needed it because they were working or because they did not have a spouse or partner to help care for the child. These results support previous findings of single mothers being more likely to use non-maternal care than two-parent families (NICHD Early Child Care Research Network, 1997). Cohabiting mothers were not significantly different from married mothers.

Summary. Approximately 37 percent of children ages 0 to 5 received some type of regular non-parental child care in Los Angeles County in 2000–2001. Child care arrangements depended on how old the child was. For example, only 22 percent of children younger than 1 year received non-parental child care compared with about 40 percent of children 1 year and older.

Although our bivariate results show that children of Latino, lower-income, and foreign-born parents were more likely to be cared for exclusively by their parents than other children, the results of the multivariate analysis suggest that these effects were due to differences in other socioeconomic (SES) characteristics, such as maternal education and employment. Once these other characteristics are held constant, Latino, low-income, and foreign-born parents were about as likely to use non-parental child care as other families.

Mothers who were employed were significantly more likely to use non-parental child care, even when other SES characteristics were held constant. Those who worked part-time are five times as likely to use non-parental child care as mothers who were not employed. Mothers employed full-time were almost 10 times as likely to use non-parental child care. However, it is important to keep in mind that the use of non-parental child care was not limited to working mothers: 17 percent of mothers who were not employed used non-parental child care.

Moreover, not all employed mothers used non-parental child care: Approximately 30 percent of children whose mothers were employed full-time received *no* non-parental child care. In many cases, these children were probably cared for by their other parent. For example, some parents are able to coordinate their work hours in order to provide full-time parental care while holding down two jobs. In other cases, mothers or fathers may care for their child while working—e.g., while running a small business or working at home. In some cases, employed parents may not be using non-parental child care because of difficulties in locating care at an affordable price. However, since L.A.FANS did not ask parents about whether or not they wanted or needed non-parental child care, these results cannot shed light directly on the unmet need for child care in Los Angeles.

Two other groups that are significantly more likely to use non-parental child care are single mothers—those who are neither married nor cohabiting—and teen mothers. Unlike married or cohabiting mothers, single mothers do not have a spouse or partner at home to help with child care. Even if a child's father sees the child occasionally or regularly, he is often not available to provide regular child care. Thus, single mothers are considerably more likely to rely on other sources of care. Teen mothers in L.A.FANS are considerably less likely to be married than older mothers (results not shown) and also more likely to be single. Most teen mothers in L.A.FANS rely on relative care, in some cases because they live with one or more of their own parents.

Number of Arrangements Used

Arranging for child care can involve employing multiple child care providers. For example, a child may go to preschool in the morning and a relative or baby-sitter in the afternoon. Arranging child care may be particularly difficult for parents who work full-time, because a particular child care providers' hours may be shorter than parents' work hours. National studies show that parents often use multiple child care arrangements at any given time (Hofferth, 1996). However, many of these studies count parental child care as a type of child care arrangement, unlike our study which focuses exclusively on non-parental care.

Figure 2[16] shows the distribution of the number of child care arrangements used by families of young children in the L.A.FANS sample, by the age of the child. Only children who received some type of non-parental child care were included in this graph. Virtually all children under age 1 had only one type of child care arrangement. The proportion having two or more arrangements increases with the child's age. However, for the total sample, 86 percent had only one child care arrangement.

Figure 2. Number of Child Care Arrangements

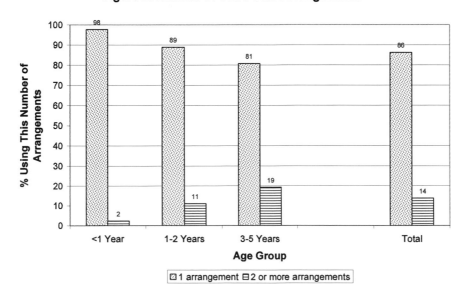

---

[16] Results in this section are based on the 348 sampled preschoolers ages 0–5 who received some type of non-parental care in the four weeks before interview.

We also examined the relationship of neighborhood, family, and child characteristics with the number of child care arrangements used. None of the associations were statistically significant, except for the child's sex. Boys are about twice as likely as girls to have more than one child care arrangement (results not shown).

Because of the predominance of using one child care arrangement, we focus in the rest of the analysis on the primary child care arrangement reported for each child, unless the text explicitly indicates otherwise.

Summary. Our results show that relatively few parents report using more than one non-parental child care arrangement for their child. Although national studies show that the use of multiple arrangements per child is common (Hofferth, 1996), those studies generally include parental care as a type of child care, unlike this study. In the rest of the report, we therefore focus on the primary type of child care each child receives, unless otherwise indicated.

Primary Type of Child Care Used

Next, we examined the primary type of care used by children who received any non-parental child care. Type of child care was divided into three categories: (1) relative-based care (care by a relative other than the child's mother and father); (2) non–relative-based care (in the child's or the sitter's home, including a regular baby-sitter, day care provider, nanny, neighbor, friend); and (3) center-based care (day care center, preschool, nursery school, or Head Start). Percentages are based on only those mothers who regularly use non-parental child care and reported which type of arrangement was used. Figure 3 shows the primary child care arrangement for children by age, for children who received any non-parental care.

Figure 3. Type of Child Care Used by Child's Age

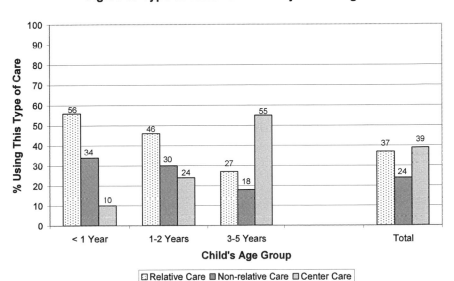

Most children (56 percent) who receive non-parental child care during their first year of life are cared for by relatives. Non-relative care is the next most common for this age group and center care is relatively uncommon (10 percent). Center care increases in frequency as children grow older. For 3- to 5-year-olds, center care is by far the most common type of non-parental child care used. For all ages combined, relative care and center care are about equally common while non-relative care is less common.

Table 5. Type of Non-Parental Child Care Used (Relative Risk Ratios Showing the Likelihood That Parents Use Relative and Non-Relative Care Rather Than Center Care)

Variable	Relative Risk Ratios	
	Relative Care	Non-Relative Care
Service Planning Area (SPA)		
Antelope Valley (SPA 1)	0.16	0.00
San Fernando (SPA 2)	**0.03**	0.16
San Gabriel (SPA 3)	**0.05**	**0.11**
Metro (SPA 4)	**0.01**	**0.06**
West (SPA 5)	**0.07**	0.32
South (SPA 6) *Reference category*	*1.00*	*1.00*
East (SPA 7)	**0.02**	**0.08**
South Bay (SPA 8)	**0.02**	0.22
Neighborhood Poverty Level		
Very poor *Reference Category*	*1.00*	*1.00*
Poor	1.73	1.49
Nonpoor	2.16	2.21
Family Income (in $10,000s)	1.01	1.03
Maternal Education		
Less than high school *Reference Category*	*1.00*	*1.00*
High school graduate	0.95	1.31
Beyond high school	0.87	0.49
College graduate	0.58	0.81
Beyond college	0.19	1.37
Employment Status		
Not employed *Reference category*	*1.00*	*1.00*
Part-time	2.01	1.46
Full-time	**3.67**	1.54
Ethnicity		
White *Reference category*	*1.00*	*1.00*
Latino	0.97	1.59
Black	**0.09**	0.22
Asian/Pacific Islander	3.77	2.03
Maternal Nativity Status		
U.S. born	0.94	1.01
Foreign born *Reference category*	*1.00*	*1.00*
Marital Status		
Married *Reference category*	*1.00*	*1.00*
Single (not married/not cohabitating)	2.44	**3.84**
Cohabitating (not married)	2.81	2.31
Teenage Mother		
Yes	0.28	**0.23**
No *Reference category*	*1.00*	*1.00*
Child's Age		
Under 1 year *Reference category*	*1.00*	*1.00*
1 to 2 years	0.29	0.49
3 to 5 years	**0.05**	**0.07**
Child's Gender		
Male	0.95	1.61
Female *Reference category*	*1.00*	*1.00*
Unweighted number of cases	348	

* Statistically significant results (at p<.05) in bold; reference categories in italics. Standard errors are adjusted for cluster by neighborhood.

To examine the relationship of neighborhood, family, and child characteristics and the type of child care used, we again use multivariate statistical analysis. In this case, we estimated a multinomial logistic regression with a dependent variable which includes three categories: relative care, non-relative care, and center care.[17] Specifically, we contrast the use of relative care and non-relative care with the use of center-based care (which is the reference or omitted category). The results are shown in Table 5 as relative risk ratios (RRRs).[18] RRRs show the relative risk that a child with a given characteristic will be in either relative care or non-relative care instead of center care. Only children who received some non-parental care are included in this analysis.

The results show that that the SPA in which a family lives is statistically significantly associated with child care type. Compared with children in SPA 6 (South), children in SPAs 3, 4, and 7 are less likely to use relative or non-relative care and, thus, more likely to use center-based care. Children in SPAs 2, 5, and 8 are also less likely to use relative care compared with those in SPA 6. These associations are all statistically significant. This regional pattern of child care utilization may be a result of differences in the characteristics of families in each SPA—although our analysis holds many key characteristics constant—or of differences in the availability of child care. Unfortunately, we do not have information on supply of child care with which to examine these hypotheses. These regional differences may be particularly important for planning expansions of child care and preschool services and merit further investigation.

Family income is not significantly associated with the type of care used once other variables are held constant. Mothers who work full-time are significantly more likely to use relative care than center care, compared with women who work part-time or are not working. This finding may be related to the circumstances under which mothers return to work after childbirth rather than to a causal effect of employment on relative care. For example, mothers who have relatives available to care for their young children may be more likely to return full-time to work earlier than other mothers. Alternatively, women who work full-time out of financial need may also rely more heavily on relatives because, as we show below, relatives are much more likely than other types of care to be free or low cost.

African-Americans are significantly *less* likely to use relative care (rather than center care) compared with white and Latino children. Asian and Pacific Islander (API) children appear more likely to use relative care than other children, but the differences between API and white children are not statistically significant. However, a separate statistical test (not shown) comparing API and African-American children shows that differences between these two groups are statistically significant, with API children being considerably more likely to use relative than center care, compared with African-American children.

Compared with married mothers, single mothers (neither married nor cohabiting) are significantly more likely to use non-relative care than center care. There are no significant differences in the coefficients for the relative care vs. center care contrast by marital status. Teen mothers are also significantly less likely to use non-relative care than center care compared with other mothers.

---

[17] The Hausman specification test was used to test for the property of independence of irrelevant alternatives, with the results indicating that this assumption was met.

[18] These ratios from a multinomial logit analysis can also be referred to as odds-ratios. The term "relative risk ratio" is used in the literature and in this report to indicate that these ratios are relative to the omitted category of the outcome variable.

A final result is that children ages 3 to 5 are significantly more likely to use center care (rather than either relative or non-relative care) compared with children under age 1. This result—added to our earlier finding that parents are less likely to use child care for infants than for older children—reflects a general preference for parental or more individualized care arrangements for very young children (Hofferth, 1996).

Summary. Among children ages 0 to 5 in L.A.FANS receiving non-parental child care, relative and center care were the most common types: 37 percent used relative care, 24 percent used non-relative care, and 39 percent use center care. The type of care used varied considerably depending on the age of the child. Relatives provide the majority (56 percent) of care for children under age 1, but centers provide the majority of care (55 percent) for older children ages 3 to 5. The results on use of non-parental care and on the type of care used suggest that families prefer to care for very young children (under age 1) by themselves, when possible. However, the prevalence of parental and relative care for very young children may also reflect greater difficulty in finding high-quality non-relative or center-based care for children in this age group.

The multivariate results show that full-time maternal employment, ethnicity, marital/cohabitation status, teen motherhood, and the child's age are significantly associated with the type of child care used. Women who work full-time are more likely to use relative care rather than center care compared with women who are not employed. African-American families appear to be more likely to use center-based care than white families, although the difference is statistically significant in the multinomial model only for the relative care vs. center care contrast. Single (non-cohabiting) mothers are more likely to use non-relative care than center care compared with married women. Teen mothers are less likely to use non-relative care. Finally, older children are significantly more likely to be in center-based care than younger children.

Surprisingly, family income was not related to the choice of type of child care. As noted above, the reason may be in part that the three types of child care used in this analysis are very broad and heterogeneous. For example, both well-off and poor families use non-relative care providers. However, the well-off families may be more likely to hire nannies, au pairs, and in-home baby-sitters, while the poor families may be more likely to rely on neighbors and friends who care for several children.

There are also a number of regional differences by SPA in the types of child care used. Compared with children in SPA 6 (South), children in other SPAs are more likely to be in center-based child care and less likely to use relative or non-relative child care—although not all of the relationships are statistically significant. This regional pattern of child care utilization may be a result of differences in the characteristics of families in each SPA—although our analysis holds many key characteristics constant—or differences in the availability of child care. These regional differences, which may be particularly important for planning expansions of child care and preschool services, merit further investigation.

Amount of Child Care Used Per Week

The amount of child care was measured as hours of child care used per week summed across all child care arrangements combined. In Figure 4,[19] we examine the amount of care used by age of the child. In this graph, part-time care is defined as using more than 0 hours and less than 30 hours of child care per week, while full-time care is defined as using 30 or more hours of child care per week.

The majority of children who receive non-parental child care receive full-time (30 hours or more per week) care. Perhaps surprisingly, children under age 1 are more likely to receive full-time child care than older children. The most likely reason is that these very young children are generally cared for by relatives or baby-sitters (non-relatives) rather than through centers (see Figure 3). Relatives and non-relatives may provide care in the baby's own home or in a homelike setting. In contrast, older children are more likely to use center-based care, which often offers more limited hours.

Figure 4. Amount of Child Care Used

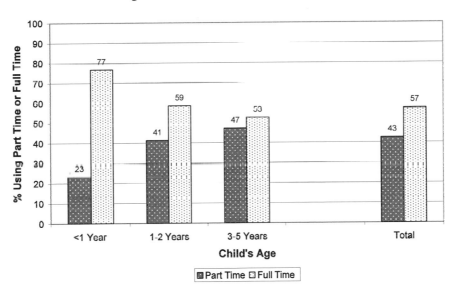

We also examine the associations between neighborhood, family, and child characteristics and the amount of child care used. In this analysis, we used multivariate logit models to examine the association of each variable with the odds of using full-time child care, i.e., whether all non-parental child care arrangement combined were 30 hours or more per week. The results are presented in Table 6.

---

[19] Results in this section are based on 315 preschoolers ages 0–5; 33 cases were dropped because they did not report the number of hours the child spent in non-parental care.

Table 6. Whether Child Receives Full-Time Child Care (30 Hours per Week or More), Based on Multivariate Logit Model

Variable	Odds-Ratios
Service Planning Area (SPA)	
Antelope and San Fernando (SPAs 1 and 2)	1.15
San Gabriel (SPA 3)	0.84
Metro (SPA 4)	1.43
West (SPA 5)	1.44
South (SPA 6) *Reference category*	*1.00*
East (SPA 7)	2.87
South Bay (SPA 8)	1.17
Neighborhood Poverty Level	
Very poor *Reference Category*	*1.00*
Poor	0.70
Nonpoor	0.50
Family Income (in $10,000s)	1.02
Maternal Education	
Less than high school *Reference Category*	*1.00*
High school graduate	0.32
Beyond high school	0.58
College graduate	0.48
Beyond college	0.62
Employment Status	
Not employed *Reference category*	*1.00*
Part-time	0.91
Full-time	**3.76**
Ethnicity	
White *Reference category*	*1.00*
Latino	0.81
Black	3.48
Asian/Pacific Islander	1.62
Maternal Nativity Status	
U.S. born	1.25
Foreign born *Reference category*	*1.00*
Marital Status	
Married *Reference category*	*1.00*
Single (not married/not cohabitating)	0.50
Cohabitating (not married)	1.61
Teenage Mother	
Yes	4.01
No *Reference category*	*1.00*
Child's Age	
Under 1 year *Reference category*	*1.00*
1 to 2 years	0.78
3 to 5 years	0.61
Child's Gender	
Male	**2.28**
Female *Reference category*	*1.00*
Unweighted number of cases	319

* Statistically significant results (at $p<.05$) in bold; reference categories in italics. Standard errors are adjusted for cluster by neighborhood.

** SPAs 1 and 2 are combined in this analysis because of the small number of cases (n=4).

Not surprisingly, mothers who worked full-time were significantly more likely to use full-time child care than mothers who were not employed or mothers who were employed part-time.

Our results also show that boys are significantly more likely to be in full-time child care than girls. None of the other variables are significantly associated with full-time vs. part-time care.

Summary. We examined the use of part-time and full-time child care. We defined full-time child care as 30 hours or more per week. For children ages 0–5 in L.A.FANS, 43 percent received part-time child care and 57 percent received full-time child care. Again, there are large variations in the amount of child care by the child's age. In this case, however, it is children under age 1 who are most likely to receive full-time child care. Among these very young children who received any non-parental child care, 77 percent received full-time care. By contrast, for 3- to 5-year-olds receiving any non-parental care, 53 percent received full-time care. These differences by age most likely reflect differences in the type of care needed by infants compared with older preschoolers. While older preschoolers may spend time with older siblings or playing with other children, infants need full-time adult care. As discussed above, most of the non-parental care for infants comes from relatives.

The results of the multivariate analysis show that mothers who are employed full-time are more likely to use full-time care for their children. Perhaps more surprising is the result that boys are more than twice as likely as girls to receive full-time child care.

Cost of Child Care

Next, we examine the amount of money that families pay for child care. The total monthly cost of child care should depend in part on the number of hours that a child is in a care arrangement. In Figures 5 and 6,[20] we present information on the cost of child care in two ways.[21] Figure 5 shows the total *monthly cost* of child care reported by the number of hours that child care was used per week. The objective of this figure is to provide an idea of how much families pay each month for child care. Figure 6 shows the cost of child care calculated in another way. For this figure, we divided the total monthly costs of each type of child care by the number of hours of care used in the preceding month to get an *hourly cost*. This figure provides a more direct comparison of the cost of each type of child care.

---

[20] Results in this section were based on 287 sampled preschoolers ages 0–5; 28 cases were dropped from the analysis because they did not report information on whether or not the family paid for child care and the cost of child care.

[21] Some mothers reported the combined total cost of child care their household pays for two or more children. For example, the family may report that they pay a nanny $400 per month to care for two children. There is no entirely satisfactory way to calculate the cost of care per child for these families in a manner that is equivalent to families paying for the care of only one child. If we divide the hourly cost of care by the number of children cared for, we are likely to underestimate what the family would have to pay for child care for one child. For example, a family is likely to pay a baby-sitter the same amount or only slightly more (but not twice as much) for two children compared with what they would have to pay for one child. Fortunately, there are only four cases of children in the sample for this study in which mothers combined costs for two or more children. We have done the tabulations in several ways and found that the calculation procedure for these children has no effect on the overall results.

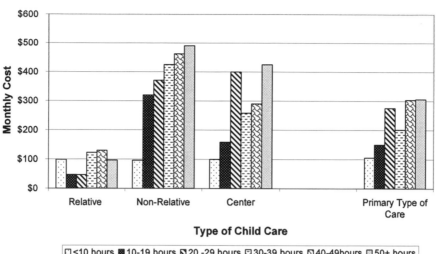

Figure 5. Monthly Cost of Child Care by Type of Care and Hours Per Week

☐ <10 hours ▨ 10-19 hours ◩ 20 -29 hours ▤ 30-39 hours ▨ 40-49hours ☐ 50+ hours

The results in Figure 5 show relative care is by far the least expensive arrangement. The reason is partly that many relatives (54 percent) provide child care at no cost and partly that when relatives are paid, the amount is generally small (on average, $239 per month). In contrast, baby-sitters, nannies, neighbors, and other non-relative care providers are the most expensive. On average, the monthly cost of a full-time (30 hours or more) non-relative provider is between $460 and $480 per month. Only about 14 percent of non-relative providers provide care at no cost. If we look only at full-time care from non-relative providers who charge for care, the average monthly cost is $531 per month. The costs of center care fall between those for relative and non-relative care. For center care, 44 percent of parents report that the child care is provided at no cost. As shown in Figure 5, full-time center care costs average between $260 and $450 per month. Families who have to pay for center care and use center care full-time pay an average of $446 per month.

Figure 6. Hourly Cost of Child Care by Type of Care

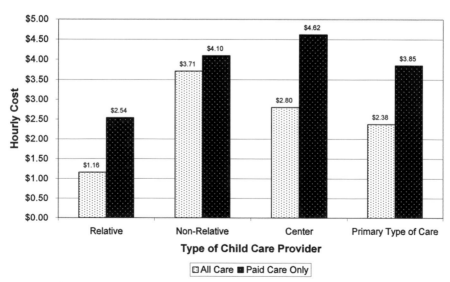

☐ All Care ■ Paid Care Only

In Figure 6, we show the hourly cost of each type of child care. The first bar in each pair shows the average hourly cost including no-cost care (i.e., care that the family pays nothing for).

34

The second bar shows the hourly cost for families who pay for care. Families who pay for care pay an average of $3.85 an hour. If we exclude no-cost care, Figure 6 shows that center care is actually more expensive per hour than non-relative care. Care provided by relatives remains the cheapest alternative.

The results in Figures 5 and 6 are indicative of one of the central dilemmas in policy debates about the availability of child care. The $400 and $500 per month cost of non-relative or center-based child care is a lot of money for many families to pay. On the other hand, average hourly amount paid for child care (even if relative care is excluded) is well below the minimum wage of $5.15 per hour.[22] Hourly costs paid by parents are likely to be lower than wages paid to non-relative and center-based child care workers both because many care for multiple children at one time and because of child care subsidies. Nonetheless, the hourly cost to parents also must cover other costs the care provider incurs (such as the non-labor costs of running a child care center).

In Figure 7, we examine the costs of child care for families at different income levels. As in Table 3, we have divided family income into quartiles for this graph.

Figure 7. Average Monthly Child Care Costs by Income Level

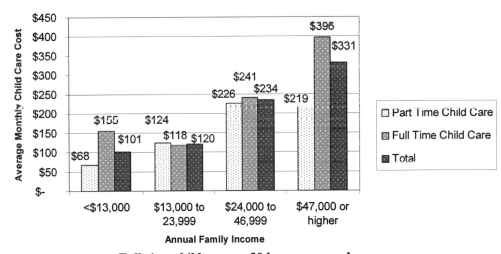

Full-time child care >= 30 hours per week

Families with lower incomes pay less for child care than more well-off families. The reason is partly that they rely more heavily on relative care than higher-income families, as shown below in Figure 8.

---

[22] For the federal and state minimum wages, see http://www.dol.gov/dol/topic/wages/minimumwage.htm. The California minimum wage for full-time work (40 hours a week) is $6.75.

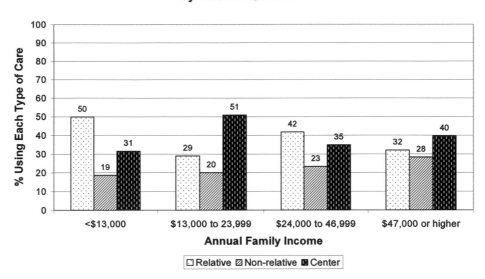

Figure 8. Percent Using Each Type of Child Care by Income Quartiles

Another reason that child care costs are lower for lower-income families is that they are more likely to have access to child care centers at no cost. For example, among families using center-based care, 57 percent of families with incomes below $13,000 and 63 percent of families with incomes between $13,000 and $24,000 reported paying nothing for this care. Almost all higher-income families had to pay for center care.

Nonetheless, for lower-income families who do not have access to no-cost or low-cost care from relatives or centers, child care can be expensive. Low-income families (annual income less than $24,000 or $2,000 per month) in the L.A.FANS sample who pay for full-time child care pay an average of $243 per month for care.

In Tables 7a and 7b, we examine two aspects of the cost of child care. Table 7a examines the relationship between socioeconomic characteristics and whether or not the family pays anything for child care. Table 7b examines the average hourly cost of care for those families who do pay for care. Both tables include payment and costs only for the primary type of child care used for each child.

In Table 7a, the outcome variable indicates whether or not the family pays for care, so the odds-ratios shown indicate the likelihood that families with a particular characteristic (e.g., Latino) will pay for child care compared with families in the omitted category (e.g., white). Perhaps surprisingly, the results show that families in SPA 5 (West), which has the highest average household income of any SPA, are significantly less likely to pay for child care than families in SPA 6 (South). Earlier analyses (not shown) indicate that on average respondents in SPA 5 are actually slightly more likely to pay for child care than those in SPA 6 *when no other variables are held constant*, although the association is not statistically significant. Once socioeconomic status is held constant, however, residents of SPA 5 are less likely to pay. We speculate that this result may be due to SPA 5 residents having greater access to free child care at work than residents of other SPAs, but it may also be true that, holding constant socioeconomic status, SPA 5 residents have greater access to or are more successful in finding free child care.

36

Less surprising is the result that women who continued their education after college and those who work full-time or part-time are significantly more likely to pay for child care. These mothers are likely to have higher earnings than more poorly educated or non-employed mothers and, therefore, to be better able to afford child care. Mothers who work part-time are significantly more likely to pay for child care than mothers working full-time. This result may reflect lack of flexibility in no-cost child care such as Head Start and subsidized center care. In addition, part-time workers are less likely to have access to no-cost employer-sponsored child care.

Families who use non-relative care and center care are significantly more likely to pay for child care than families who rely on relatives for child care, even when socioeconomic variables are held constant. As Figure 6 shows, a substantial proportion of relatives provides care for free or low cost. Free care is considerably rarer in child care centers and rarer still among non-relative care arrangements. The results show that families are most likely to pay if they use non-relative care and paying for child care is statistically significantly more likely for non-relative than for center care.

Table 7b is based on the sample of families who report paying for child care.[23] In contrast to previous multivariate results shown in the above tables, results in this table are based on an ordinary least squares (OLS) regression model (often referred to as multiple regression). The interpretation of the numbers is Table 7b is different from those in earlier tables. In this case, the regression coefficients refer to the number of dollars that the cost of child care would increase or decrease with a change in one of the socioeconomic variables. For example, Table 7b shows that the average hourly cost of child care is $2.55 lower for full-time care than for part-time care.

---

[23] The analysis in Table 7b is based on the 198 sampled preschoolers for whom we have hours and cost information and whose families paid for child care.

Table 7a. Socioeconomic Variables and the Cost of Child Care: Whether Family Pays Anything for Care

Variable	Whether Family Pays *Anything* for Child Care (Odds Ratios)
Service Planning Area (SPA) [Reference category: SPA6]	
Antelope and San Fernando (SPAs 1 and 2)	0.34
San Gabriel (SPA 3)	2.52
Metro (SPA 4)	0.75
West (SPA 5)	**0.10**
East (SPA 7)	0.60
South Bay (SPA 8)	0.81
Neighborhood Poverty Level [Reference category: Very poor]	
Poor	0.34
Nonpoor	0.72
Family Income (in $10,000s)	1.01
Maternal Education [Reference category: Less than high school]	
High school graduate	1.28
Beyond high school	1.94
College graduate	1.95
Beyond college	**8.96**
Employment Status [Reference category: Not employed]	
Part-time	**15.20**
Full-time	**5.61**
Ethnicity [Reference category: White]	
Latino	0.72
Black	0.46
Asian/Pacific Islander	0.45
Maternal Nativity Status [Reference category: Foreign born]	
U.S. born	2.23
Marital Status [Reference category: Married]	
Single (not married/not cohabitating)	1.42
Cohabitating (not married)	1.96
Teenage Mother [Reference category: No]	
Yes	1.47
Child's Age [Reference category: Under 1 year]	
1 to 2 years	2.44
3 to 5 years	1.17
Child's Gender [Reference category: Female]	
Male	0.59
Type of Child Care [Reference category: Relative care]	
Non-relative care	**23.41**
Center care	**8.13**
Amount of Child Care [Reference category.: Part-time]	
Full-time	1.06
Unweighted number of cases	287

* Results from logit regression model. Statistically significant results at p<.05 in bold. Standard errors are adjusted for cluster by neighborhood.

** SPAs 1 and 2 combined in this analysis because of the small number of cases in SPA 1 (n=4).

Table 7b. Socioeconomic Variables and the Cost of Child Care: Hourly Cost for Families Who Pay

Variable	*Amount* Family Pays for Child Care (OLS Regression Coefficients)
Service Planning Area (SPA) *[Reference category: SPA6]*	
Antelope and San Fernando (SPAs 1 and 2)	1.07
San Gabriel (SPA 3)	0.92
Metro (SPA 4)	0.19
West (SPA 5)	2.64
East (SPA 7)	0.17
South Bay (SPA 8)	0.16
Neighborhood Poverty Level *[Reference category: Very poor]*	
Poor	-0.27
Nonpoor	0.43
Family Income (in $10,000s)	0.01
Maternal Education *[Reference category: Less than high school]*	
High school graduate	-0.16
Beyond high school	0.01
College graduate	2.39
Beyond college	0.61
Employment Status *[Reference category: Not employed]*	
Part-time	1.17
Full-time	0.25
Ethnicity *[Reference category: White]*	
Latino	-0.41
Black	-0.02
Asian/Pacific Islander	-0.56
Maternal Nativity Status *[Reference category: Foreign born]*	
U.S. born	0.71
Marital Status *[Reference category: Married]*	
Single (not married/not cohabitating)	-0.53
Cohabitating (not married)	**-1.08**
Teenage Mother *[Reference category: No]*	
Yes	0.70
Child's Age *[Reference category: Under 1 year]*	
1 to 2 years	-2.41
3 to 5 years	-2.01
Child's Gender *[Reference category: Female]*	
Male	-0.05
Type of Child Care *[Reference category: Relative care]*	
Non-relative care	0.89
Center care	-0.14
Amount of Child Care *[Reference category.: Part-time]*	
Full-time	**-2.55**
Unweighted number of cases	198

* Results from OLS regression model. Statistically significant results at p<.05 in bold. Standard errors are adjusted for cluster by neighborhood.

** SPAs 1 and 2 are combined in this analysis because of the small number of cases in SPA 1 (n=4).

The results in Table 7b show that only two variables are statistically significantly related to the cost of child care for families who pay. The first is whether the child care is full-time (30 hours a week or more) or whether it is part-time (less than 30 hours per week). As noted above, the hourly cost of full-time child care is significantly lower than part-time care. Combined with the finding in Table 7a that women who work part-time are significantly more likely to pay for care than those who work part-time, these results suggest that it is considerably more difficult to find low-cost care for families needing part-time compared with full-time care. As discussed in the final section of this report, we believe that these results highlight the importance of including high-quality, low-cost part-time child care with flexible hours in future policy initiatives to expand child care.

The other significant result in this analysis is that parents in cohabiting households pay lower hourly child care costs compared with married couples. Cohabiting couples have fewer financial resources and are younger than married couples. Although age and family income are held constant in the results shown in Table 7b, it is possible that other aspects of age and socioeconomic status that are not well measured by the age and family income variables account for this result. For example, cohabiting mothers may be less likely to receive help in paying for child care from their partners than married mothers do from husbands.

Summary. Our results show that child care can be a substantial portion of families' budgets. For example, families with an annual income of $13,000 or less who use full-time non-parental child care pay an average of $155 per month in child care costs. The comparable average monthly cost is $118 for families with incomes of $13,000 to $23,999; $241 for families with incomes of $24,000 to $46,999; and $396 for families with incomes of $47,000 and higher. These average costs would be considerably higher, except that a substantial proportion of families, particularly in the lower-income groups, receive child care at no cost.

Relative care is by far the least expensive type of child care. More than half of relative-provided child care is provided at no cost, but when parents pay relatives to care for their children, they pay an average of $2.54 per hour compared with $4.10 and $4.62 per hour for non-relative and center-based care.

Our multivariate results show that families are significantly more likely to pay for child care (as opposed to receiving it at no cost) if the mother has education beyond college, is employed, and is using care providers other than relatives. Moreover, families are significantly more likely to have to pay for part-time than for full-time child care. For families who do pay for child care, the multivariate results show that those who use full-time child care pay significantly less than those who use part-time care. Both the greater need to pay for part-time care and its higher hourly cost suggest that finding and paying for part-time care is more difficult for families that need it.

Child-Adult Ratios

Mothers in L.A.FANS were asked to report on the number of children being cared for and the number of adults providing the care in each child care arrangement used. As noted above, this measure of child care quality does not take into account many aspects of quality including whether child care activities include stimulating environments and activities which help children develop cognitive, social, and academic skills (e.g., number and letter recognition). For example, the ratios of children to adults are generally higher in high-quality child care centers than in most relative care arrangements (since relative care ratios are so low). Yet high-quality child care may provide significant care, socialization, and learning advantages, especially for older preschoolers, over the average relative care arrangement.

Figure 9[24] presents the child-to-adult ratios for the primary child care arrangement for each child by the child's age and type of care. The results show that the ratios for relative care are less than 2 children per adult for all age groups. In fact, in some relative arrangements, there are more adults present than children. The maximum number of children per adults reported for

Figure 9. Ratio of Children to Adults in Primary Child Care Arrangements

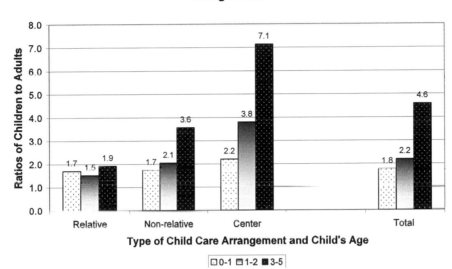

relative care is five children per adult. There is considerably more variation by children's age in the child-adult ratios for non-relatives and centers. For children under age 2, the ratios in non-relative care are about 2 children per adult or less. For 3- to 5-year-olds, non-relative providers are caring for an average of 4 children. Centers average just above 2 children per adult for children under age 1. The average increases to 3.8 for 1- to 2-year-olds and to just over 7 for 3- to 5-year-olds.

For comparison, child care centers which are funded by the California Department of Education under Title 5 are required to have a maximum child-adult ratio of 3 for infants from birth to 18 months, 4 for toddlers ages 18 to 36 months, and 8 for children age 36 months or older.[25]

Figure 10 shows child-adults ratios by type of child care arrangement and family income level. Ratios for relative care are about the same regardless of family income. However, there is considerable variation in the ratios for non-relative care: The ratio for the poorest children averages 5.4 children per adult compared with averages of 1.9 to 2.7 for families with higher incomes.

The ratios for center care show that the highest-income families' children are in centers with the highest ratio of children to adults.

---

[24] Results reported in this section are based on the 287 sampled preschoolers for whom parents reported all variables. This subsample is the same as that included in the section on child care costs above.
[25] Section 18290 of Title 5 of the California Code of Regulations, available at www.dss.cahwnet.gov/getinfo/pdf/ccc4.pdf.

Figure 10. Ratio of Children to Adults by Child Care Type and Family Income

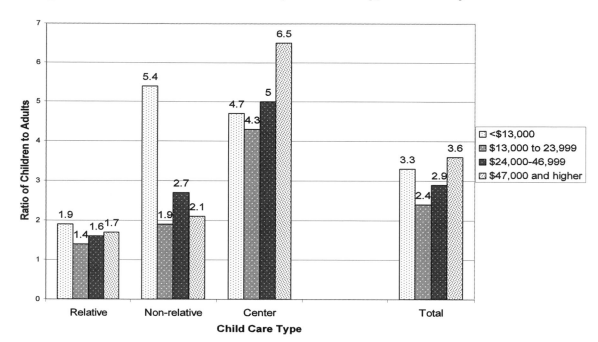

In Table 8, we examine the association of neighborhood, family, and child variables and type and cost of care with the child-adult ratio in the child's primary care arrangement, using multivariate statistical analysis. Here we again use multivariate regression, which is also known as ordinary least squares (OLS) regression. The results show that, compared with children in very poor neighborhoods, those in poor neighborhoods have significantly lower child-adult ratios in their child care arrangements as well. Family income is also a significant factor: Higher family income is significantly associated with lower child-adult ratios. The coefficient indicates that for each increase of $10,000 in family income, the child-adult ratio decreases by 0.4 children per adult. This result suggests that, even holding constant other socioeconomic characteristics, children in poor families are in higher child-adult ratio child care than other children.

Not surprisingly, older children are in child care with significantly higher child-adult ratios than younger children. This makes sense both because younger children need more attention and because the state-mandated child-adult ratios are higher for older than for younger children. Center

Table 8. Association of Socioeconomic Variables with the Child-Adult Ratio at Primary Care Arrangement

Variable	OLS Regression Coefficients
Service Planning Area (SPA) *[Reference category: SPA 6]*	
Antelope and San Fernando (SPAs 1 and 2)	0.95
San Gabriel (SPA 3)	0.34
Metro (SPA 4)	-0.32
West (SPA 5)	0.37
East (SPA 7)	0.52
South Bay (SPA 8)	-0.01
Neighborhood Poverty Level *[Reference category: Very poor]*	
Poor	**-0.86**
Nonpoor	-0.50
Family Income (in $10,000s)	**-0.03**
Maternal Education *[Reference category: Less than high school]*	
High school graduate	-0.17
Beyond high school	-0.05
College graduate	0.61
Beyond college	0.28
Employment Status *[Reference category: Not employed]*	
Part-time	-0.78
Full-time	-0.45
Ethnicity *[Reference category: White]*	
Latino	-0.48
Black	-1.41
Asian/Pacific Islander	-0.93
Maternal Nativity Status *[Reference category: Foreign born]*	
U.S. born	0.26
Marital Status *[Reference category: Married]*	
Single (not married/not cohabiting)	0.49
Cohabitating (not married)	0.40
Teenage Mother *[Reference category: No]*	
Yes	-1.74
Child's Age *[Reference category: Under 1 year]*	
1 to 2 years	0.08
3 to 5 years	**1.43**
Child's Gender *[Reference category: Female]*	
Male	-0.08
Type of Child Care *[Reference category: Relative care]*	
Non-relative care	**0.66**
Center care	**3.25**
Hourly Cost of Child Care *[Reference category: No cost]*	
$1.50 to $2.50/hour	0.16
$2.50 to $5.00/hour	**0.81**
$5.00/hour and higher	0.62
Constant	1.98
Unweighted number of cases	287

* Results from OLS regression model. Statistically significant results (at p<.05) in bold; reference categories in italics. Standard errors are adjusted for cluster by neighborhood.

care is associated with significantly higher ratios compared with relative care. At the same time, non-relative care is associated with significantly lower child-adult ratios.

The results show some significant association between child-adult ratios and the cost of care.[26] Specifically, children in families who pay between $2.50 and $5.00 per hour have child care arrangements with significantly lower child-adult ratios than families that pay nothing for child care. Nonetheless, the relationship is not as strong or consistent as might be expected. The reason may be that each of our three categories of child care is fairly heterogeneous. For example, non-relative care providers may include mothers who care for a neighbor's child in their own home to well-trained and comparatively well-paid nannies caring for one child. For licensed child care, state regulation of child-adult ratios and subsidies for child care may also play an important role in attenuating the relationship between cost and child-adult ratios.

Summary. We assessed child care quality using child-to-adult caretaker ratios for child care arrangements. As described above, these ratios have considerable limitations as indicators of child care quality. However, our analysis of these ratios produced several interesting results. On average, child-adult ratios are substantially higher for center-based care than for relative care. Non-relative care ratios are also higher than those for relative arrangements, but considerably below ratios for centers. An examination of the ratios by type of care and family income (Figure 10) illustrated the diversity in the care environments within each type of care category. For example, for non-relative care, children from the poorest families were in arrangements with an average of 5.4 children per adult caretaker, whereas children from families earning more than $47,000 per year were in arrangements with ratios of 2.1. We speculate that the difference is that non-relative arrangements used by poor families are more likely to be neighbors or other adults who take care of multiple children in their home while non-relative arrangements for higher-income families may be more likely to be nannies or baby-sitters responsible only for one or two children. On the other hand, child care centers used by the highest-income group have higher child-adult ratios than those used by the lowest-income group.

Our multivariate results show that younger children and those in higher-income families are more likely to have low child-adult ratios. Holding other factors constant, we found that child-adult ratios are highest for center care and lowest for non-relative care. The cost of child care is significantly related to child-adult ratios, but the association is not as strong or consistent as might have been expected.

---

[26] We tried several different specifications of this model (e.g., including child care costs as a continuous variable and including interactions between type of child care and costs). In general, our results showed that hourly costs were not statistically significantly associated with child-to-adult ratios.

CHAPTER FOUR
How Do Poorer Families Pay for Child Care?

A key policy issue for First 5 LA and other organizations interested in expanding child care and early childhood education options is what lower-income families currently do about child care and how they pay for it. Although the L.A.FANS data cover the period from 2000 to 2001, they provide a more recent picture of child care arrangement for the poor in Los Angeles County than any other data of which we are aware.

In this chapter, we draw together evidence presented in Chapter Three and additional information from L.A.FANS to provide a brief assessment of how lower-income families (those who earn less than $24,000 per year) pay for child care. The cut point of $24,000 was chosen to represent roughly the bottom third of the family income distribution in Los Angeles County. Although just over one-third of all families have incomes below $24,000, 45 percent of preschoolers ages 0 to 5 live in families with annual incomes below $24,000,[27] reflecting the fact that children are more likely to live in poor families on average than adults.

Another way to put these income levels into perspective is to compare them to the average cost of child care, which Figure 6 shows is $3.85 per hour. These results are shown in Figure 11.

Figure 11.
Percent of Annual Income Required to Pay Average Full Time Child Care Costs

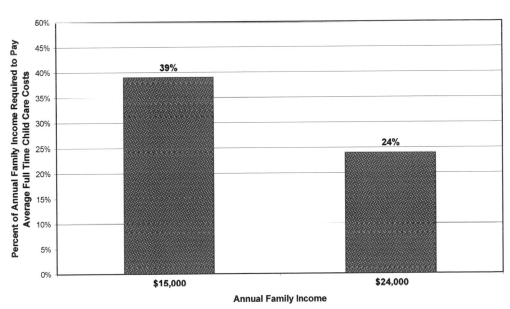

---

[27] The income figures for Los Angeles County families and families with preschoolers ages 0 to 5 are based on weighted tabulations from L.A.FANS.

If a family used child care 30 hours per week for 50 weeks per year, this would bring the average annual cost of child care to $5,775. This figure is almost one-quarter of the annual income for a family making $24,000. However, most families in our low-income category make less than $24,000 per year. Instead, they average about $15,000. For families who made this average income, $5,775 in child care costs would comprise a huge 39 percent of their total annual income. Clearly, average child care costs are out of the reach of many families who have annual incomes of $24,000 or less.

What do these families do about child are? As shown in Figure 12, one important difference between lower- and higher-income families is that mothers in lower-income families are considerably less likely to work. While approximately three-quarters of mothers in families with incomes less than $24,000 were not employed, the comparable percentage for families with incomes above $47,000 is 34 percent. The relationship between family income and maternal work is complex. In some families, parents may decide to forgo the mother's income so that she can stay home and care for the children. Therefore, their family income is lower than it would be if the mother was employed. In other families, mothers may choose not to work because the cost of child care is so high relative to their potential earnings that it would not be worthwhile. Or they may have trouble finding child care of acceptable quality. In any event, most mothers in poor families who have preschool children do not work and therefore can provide their own child care.

Figure 12:
Percent of Mothers Who Are _Not_ Employed by Family Income Category

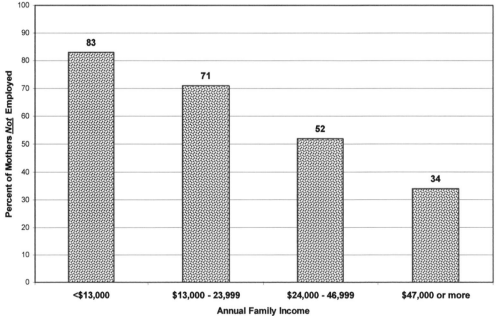

A second important factor is heavy reliance on relative care. In poorer families who do use child care, half rely on relative care (see Figure 8). Most relative caretakers provide care at no cost, but those who charge for care are paid considerably less than non-relatives, as shown in Figure 13. For example, families with annual incomes of less than $24,000 who pay for child care pay an average of $2.48 per hour for relatives compared with $2.75 for non-relatives.

For low-income families who do not use relatives for child care, most (69 percent) use center-based care. Most low-income families (77 percent) using center-based care report paying nothing for this care. Those who do pay for center care pay an average of $1.96 per hour (Figure 13), which is considerably lower than the average cost of center-based care ($4.62 per hour). The difference suggests that lower-income families who pay for center care often do so at a subsidized cost. However, the lower cost may also be due to poorer families choosing lower-cost (and perhaps lower-quality) child care centers compared with higher-income families.

The remainder of low-income families using child care (31 percent) use non-relative care. It is considerably rarer for non-relatives to provide care for free compared with relatives and center providers. Only about 21 percent of low-income families report paying nothing for non-relative care. As shown in Figure 13, those who have to pay for it pay an average of $2.75 per hour. As in the case of center-based care, this hourly rate is well below the average rate for non-relative care of $4.10.

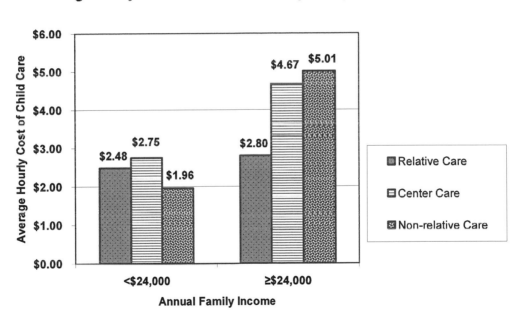

Figure 13.
Average Hourly Cost Paid for Child Care by Family Income

L.A.FANS asked all parents using child care if anyone outside their household helped to pay for child care. Among low-income families, 22 percent reported that they received some assistance, the most common source of which was a social service or welfare agency. By comparison, only 7 percent of families with incomes of $47,000 or greater reported receiving outside assistance. However, some families who report receiving a subsidy paid nothing for care and others had to pay something for care. When information on the cost of care and receipt of subsidies is combined, the picture is as follows: Among families with annual incomes less than $24,000 who use child care, 39 percent report paying nothing for child care, 7 percent report paying but receiving a subsidy, and 54 percent report paying for care and not receiving any subsidy.

In summary, many poor families do not have to use child care because mothers stay home.[28] Those who do use child care rely heavily on relatives who provide care at no or low cost. Low-income families also depend on free or subsidized care for their children. However, more than half of poor families who use child care report paying for care and not receiving any subsidy. Clearly, lower-income families who have relatives able to care for children close by or who can obtain subsidized child care have a clear advantage over other lower-income families seeking child care.

Summary. We examined child care use by the poorest families in the L.A.FANS sample— those with annual incomes of less than $24,000. One important difference between lower- and higher-income families is that mothers in poor families are considerably less likely to work. While approximately three-quarters of mothers in the poorest families were not employed, the comparable percentage for families with incomes above $47,000 was 34 percent. Those who do use non-parental child care rely heavily on relatives who provide care at no or low cost. Low-income families also are more likely to have free or subsidized care for their children. However, more than half of the poorest families who use child care report paying for care and not receiving any subsidy.

---

[28] However, children whose mothers are not employed also sometimes receive child care.

CHAPTER FIVE
Conclusions

In this report we examine several major areas of child care use among preschoolers ages 0 to 5: use of non-parental child care, primary type of child care used, amount of child care used per week, number of arrangements, the cost of care, and child-to-adult ratios in child care settings. We investigated the relationships between these child care measures and neighborhood, family, and child characteristics in Los Angeles County. Our objective has been to describe patterns of child care use in Los Angeles for policymakers and community groups who seek to expand child care and early childhood education. Below we discuss key findings.

In Los Angeles County, non-parental child care was used in 2000–2001 by only a minority (37 percent) of children ages 0 to 5 who were not yet in kindergarten or school. Among the target group for universal preschool (UPS) initiatives—i.e., children ages 3 to 5—only 39 percent received any type of non-parental child care. Moreover, among those who did receive non-parental child care, 39 percent of 0- to 5-year-old preschoolers and 55 percent of 3- to 5-year-old preschoolers were in center-based care (including preschools). These figures imply that only 14 percent of 0- to 5-year-old preschoolers and 21 percent of 3- to 5-year-old preschoolers attended child care centers at the time of the survey.

If these figures continue to characterize preschoolers in 2004–2005—as seems likely—than less than one-quarter of the target age group for UPS is currently in center care. UPS is intended to be a voluntary program. However, if UPS succeeds in attracting and providing preschools for even half of the four-year-olds in Los Angeles County, it will be a very major change in the experiences of young children and their families.

Three key results from this study suggest that initiatives such as UPS and expansion of high-quality, developmentally oriented child care programs may be especially important for children from poorer families. First, the results show that children in poor families were even less likely than other children to attend child care centers, despite the availability of subsidized care. The reason is that children in poorer families were much less likely to receive *any type* of non-parental child care and more likely to be cared for by their parents. In fact, for children in non-parental care, those in poor families are slightly *more* likely to be in center care than other children as Figure 8 shows.[29] But because so many children from poor families were cared for exclusively by parents, only 8 percent of 3- to 5-year-olds in poor families[30] attend center care compared with 21 percent of all 3- to 5-year-olds. Compounding this low percentage is the fact that not all child care centers provide early childhood education and poor children may be less likely to attend those that do—although this is an issue that we were unable to examine in the report. Thus, poorer children are considerably less likely to take advantage of the potential developmental advantages of center care and preschool, despite evidence suggesting that early childhood education may be particularly important for these children (Phillips et al., 1994; Howes and James, 2002; Currie, 2000).

Second, children who received exclusively parental care were more likely to have mothers with lower educational attainment than children who participated in non-parental care. The results

---

[29] Although the difference is small and not statistically significant.
[30] Defined here as families with annual incomes of less than $24,000 per year.

of the multivariate analysis in Table 4 show that the effects of mother's educational attainment on use of non-parental child care are not statistically significant. However, earlier analyses (not shown) showed that maternal education is strongly associated with use of non-parental care, but its effects become non-significant when maternal employment and family income—two variables highly correlated with maternal education—are held constant. This means that poor children who were cared for exclusively by their parents were more likely, on average, to have poorly educated mothers. Results from our earlier analyses of L.A.FANS showed that more poorly educated mothers are less likely to read to their children, to have books in the household, and to provide other important early learning experiences (Lara-Cinisomo and Pebley, 2003).

Third, the results also suggest that poor families who did use child care were likely to have had a difficult time paying for it. More than half of poor families (annual income less than $24,000) who used child care reported having to pay for care and not receiving any subsidy. On average, poor families paid $2.47 per hour or the equivalent of $3,705 for full-time[31] care per year. Since most families in this low-income category made considerably less than $24,000 per year, the cost of child care was likely to have been a substantial financial burden. Expansion of free UPS and free or subsidized child care would considerably reduce the burden on poor families of using child care. It may also increase the chances that mothers of preschoolers are able to work if free or low-cost high-quality child care were readily available.

Our results also show that, with two exceptions, child care use patterns do not differ significantly by ethnicity or maternal nativity. One exception is that Latino children were significantly less likely than whites to receive any non-parental child care. This difference may indicate a cultural preference for children to be cared for by their mothers, barriers (such as language and legal status) in accessing child care, or less accessibility of child care in heavily Latino neighborhoods. This result warrants further investigation. The other exception is that African-American children were considerably more likely to use center care than relative care when compared with white children. Contrary to conventional wisdom and the traditional importance of African-American grandparents in caring for grandchildren (Pebley and Rudkin, 1999), African-American children in Los Angeles were *less* likely to be cared for by relatives than to be in a child care center, compared with whites.

Two additional issues that we were not able to address directly in this report are the availability of child care slots and demand for child care slots in Los Angeles County. In the case of availability, data on child care slots are not currently available for the neighborhoods in which L.A.FANS was conducted. However, even if these data were available, measuring child care availability is especially difficult because of the importance of unlicensed providers and relatives—who are nearly impossible to count—in many communities. Our results do suggest, however, that there may have been significant regional differentials in the availability of child care. Specifically, we found large and significant variation among SPAs in the type of child care a family chose, even when socioeconomic and other characteristics are held constant. We speculate that this variation is likely to be at least partly due to regional variations in availability of different types of child care.

In the case of demand for child care in Los Angeles County, we were able to investigate actual use of child care, i.e., demand that has been met, but not unmet demand. For example, we do not know whether families who use exclusively parental child care would use non-parental care if it were

---

[31] Full-time is defined as 30 hours per week and 50 weeks per year.

available, of high quality, and affordable. Understanding both met and unmet demand for child care is essential for adequate planning for UPS and child care expansion initiatives and deserves careful investigation in future studies.

Primary Child Care Questions in L.A.FANS

1. [*Asked of children who are not yet enrolled in kindergarten or first grade*] I'd like to talk with you about all child care your child has received on a regular basis during the past four weeks from someone other than you and his/her other parent. This does not include occasional baby-sitting or backup care providers, but does include any nursery school or preschool that your child may attend.

> Has your child received care from someone other than you or his/her other parent on a regular basis during the past four weeks? [Yes/No]

2. How many different regular child care arrangements have you had for your child in the past four weeks?

3. Let's start with the person or center that provided the most care during the past four weeks. Who provided this care for your child? Who provided the next most common care? Who provided the next most common care? [*Asked about up to a maximum of three arrangements.*]

4. [*If Head Start is not already among the three most common arrangements mentioned*]: In the last four weeks, did your child attend Head Start?

For child care arrangements involving relatives:

- Does this relative who provides child care live in this household?
- Does this relative care for your child in your home or another home?
- When did this relative first start taking care of your child? What month and year?
- In the past four weeks, how many days has this relative taken care of your child?
- Think about the days in the past four weeks when this relative took care of your child. About how many hours per day, on average, did this relative care for your child on these days?
- Is this relative paid to take care of your child?
- How much is this relative paid to take care of your child?
- Including your child, how many children in total does this relative usually care for at one time?
- Does this relative care for your child/these children by (herself/himself) usually, or are there others that help?
- How many people usually care for your child/these children at a time, including this relative?

For child care arrangements involving non-relatives:

- Does this non-relative who provides child care live in this household?
- Does this non-relative care for your child in your home or another home?
- When did this non-relative first start taking care of your child? What month and year?
- In the past four weeks, how many days has this non-relative taken care of your child?

- Think about the days in the past four weeks when this non-relative took care of your child. About how many hours per day, on average, did this non-relative care for your child on these days?
- Is this non-relative paid to take care of your child?
- How much is this non-relative paid to take care of your child?
- Including your child, how many children in total does this non-relative usually care for at one time?
- Does this non-relative care for your child/these children by (herself/himself) usually, or are there others that help?
- How many people usually care for your child/these children at a time, including this non-relative?

For center-based child care (including Head Start):

- Where is this center located? Is it in a church or synagogue, a school, a community center, its own building, or some other place?
- When did your child first start attending this center? In what month and year?
- In the past four weeks, how many days did your child attend this center?
- Think about the days in the past four weeks when your child went to this center. About how many hours per day, on average, did your child spend at this center on these days?
- Is there a charge or fee for this center, paid either by you or someone else?
- How much is the fee or charge?
- Including your child, how many children at the same time are usually in your child's room or group at this center?
- How many adults are usually in your child's room or group at the same time, at this center?

Bibliography

Andrade, Jane Carroll, "Kindergarten May Be Too Late: Recognizing the Strong Connection Between a Child's Early Development and Success Later in Life, States Are Funding Preschool Programs for 4- and Even 3-Year-Olds." *State Legislatures*, 28(6):24(4), 2002.

Bradley, R. H., and R. F. Corwyn, "Socioeconomic Status and Child Development," *Annual Review of Psychology*, Vol. 53, 2002, pp. 371–399.

Brooks-Gunn, J., and G. Duncan, "The Effects of Poverty on Children," *The Future of Children*, Vol. 7, 1997, pp. 55–71.

California Department of Education, "Child Care and Development Programs," at http://www.cde.ca.gov/sp/cd/op/cdprograms.asp (accessed July 29, 2004), 2004.

Currie, J., "Early Childhood Intervention Programs: What Do We Know?" at www.jcpr.org/wpfiles/currie_EARLY_CHILDHOOD.PDF, 2000.

Duncan, G.J., et al., "Modeling the Impacts of Child Care Quality on Children's Preschool Cognitive Development," *Child Development*, Vol. 74, No. 5, 2003, pp. 1454–1475.

Federal Interagency Forum on Child and Family Statistics, "America's Children: Key National Indicators of Well-Being, 2004," at http://www.childstats.gov/americaschildren/index.asp (accessed July 29, 2004), 2004.

Fuller, B., S. W. Boots, E. Castilla, and D. Hirshberg, "A Stark Plateau—California Families See Little Growth in Child Care Centers," Policy Analysis for California Education (PACE) Policy Brief, University of California, Berkeley, available at http://pace/berkeley.edu, 2002.

Fuller, B., and D. Shih-Cheng Huang, "Targeting Investments for Universal Preschool," Policy Analysis for California Education (PACE) Policy Brief, University of California, Berkeley, available at http://pace/berkeley.edu, 2003.

Gordon, Rachel A., and P. L. Chase-Lansdale, "Availability of Child Care in the United States: A Description and Analysis of Data Sources," *Demography*, Vol. 38, No. 2, 2001, pp. 299–316.

Herszenhorn, David M., "Making a List and Checking It As School Funds Are Awaited," *New York Times*, Mar 30, 2004, p. B4.

Hofferth, Sandra L., "Child Care in the United States Today," *The Future of Children*, Vol. 6, No. 2, 1996, pp. 41–61.

Hofferth, Sandra L., and D. A. Wissoker, "Price, Quality, and Income in Child Care Choice," *The Journal of Human Resources*, Vol. 27, 1992, pp. 70–111.

Howes, C., and C. E. Hamilton, "Child Care for Young Children," in *Handbook of Research on the Education of Young Children*, B. Spodek, ed., New York: Macmillan, 1993.

Howes, C., and J. James, "Children's Social Development Within the Socialization Context of Childcare and Early Childhood Education," in Peter K. Smith and Craig H. Hart, eds., *Blackwell Handbook of Childhood Social Development*, Blackwell Handbooks of Developmental Psychology, Malden, Mass.: Blackwell Publishers, 2002, pp. 137–155.

Jacobson, L., D. Hirshberg, K. Malaske-Samu, B. B. Cuthbertson, and E. Burr, "Understanding Child Care Demand and Supply Issues: New Lessons from Los Angeles," Policy Analysis for California Education (PACE) Policy Brief, University of California, Berkeley, available at http://pace/berkeley.edu, 2001.

Lara-Cinisomo, S., and A. R. Pebley, "Los Angeles County Young Children's Literacy Experiences, Emotional Well-Being and Skills Acquisition: Results for the Los Angeles Family and Neighborhood Survey," Santa Monica, Calif.: RAND, RAND Labor and Population Working Paper Series 03-19, DRU-3041-LAFANS, 2003.

Loeb, S., B. Fuller, S. L. Kagan, and B. Carrol, "Child Care in Poor Communities: Early Learning Effects of Type, Quality, and Stability," *Child Development*, Vol. 75, No. 1, 2004, pp. 47–65.

Malaske-Samu, K., and A. Muranaka, "Child Care Counts: An Analysis of the Supply and Demand for Early Care and Educational Service in Los Angeles County," A project of the Los Angeles County Child Care Planning Committee, 2000.

McCrary, Joseph, and Stephen E. Condrey, "The Georgia Lottery: Assessing Its Administrative, Economic, and Political Effects," *The Review of Policy Research*, Vol. 20, No. 4, 2003, pp. 691(21).

McLanahan, S., and G. Sandefur, *Growing up with a Single Parent: What Hurts, What Helps,"* Cambridge, Mass.: Harvard University Press, 1994.

National Research Council, *Eager to Learn: Educating Our Preschoolers,* Barbara T. Bowman, M. Suzanne Donovan, and M. Susan Burns, eds., Commission on Behavioral and Social Sciences and Education, Washington, D.C.: National Academy Press, 2001. Available online at www.nap.edu/books/0309068363/html/.

Naybal, Rebecca, Los Angeles County Children's Planning Council, Personal Communication based on tabulations from the SF-1 file for the 2000 U.S. Census on 3- and 4-year-olds enrolled in educational programs, 2004.

NICHD Early Child Care Research Network, "Familial Factors Associated with the Characteristics of Nonmaternal Care for Infants," *Journal of Marriage and the Family,* 59:389–408, 1997.

O'Sullivan, R., A. D'Agostino, B. Page, A. Germuth, S. Heinemeier, and A. Anderson, "Child Care Initiative Phase I Evaluation," University of North Carolina, School of Education. First 5 LA Report, 2002.

Pebley, A. R., and L. Rudkin, "Grandparents Caring for Grandchildren: What Do We Know?" *Journal of Family Issues*, Vol. 20, No. 2, 1999, pp. 218–242.

Peth-Pierce, R., *The NICHD Study of Early Child Care*, NICHD Health Information and Media Publications. Available at www.nichd.nih.gov/publications/pubs/early_child_care.htm, 1998.

Phillips, D. A., M. Voran, E. Kisker, C. Howes, et al., "Child Care for Children in Poverty: Opportunity or Inequity?" *Child Development*, Vol. 65, No. 2, 1994, pp. 472–492.

Sampson, R. J., J. D. Morenoff, and T. Gannon-Rowley, "Assessing 'Neighborhood Effects': Social Processes and New Directions in Research," *Annual Review of Sociology*, Vol. 28, 2002, pp. 1–51.

Sastry, N., B. Ghosh-Dastidar, J. Adams, and A. R. Pebley, *The Design of a Multilevel Longitudinal Survey of Children, Families, and Communities: The Los Angeles Family and Neighborhoods Survey,* Santa Monica, Calif.: RAND, DRU-2400/1-LAFANS, 2003. Available at www.rand.org/labor/DRU/DRU2400.1.pdf.

Shonkoff, J., and Deborah A. Phillips, eds., *From Neurons to Neighborhoods: The Science of Early Childhood Development,* National Academy of Science/National Research Council, Committee on Integrating the Science of Early Childhood Development, Board on Children, Youth, and Families, Washington, D.C.: National Academy Press, 2000. Available at http://www.nap.edu/books/0309069882/html/.

Smith, Kristin, "Who's Minding the Kids? Child Care Arrangements," *Current Population Reports*, P70-70, Washington, D.C.: U.S. Bureau of the Census, 2000.